ANGELS IN T[...]
An Antholog[y ...]

ANGELS IN THE SUSSEX AIR
An Anthology of Sussex Poets

Selected and Edited
by
Patrick Garland

Preface by the
Duke of Richmond and Gordon

with illustrations by
David Goodman

SINCLAIR-STEVENSON

First published in Great Britain in 1995
by Sinclair-Stevenson
an imprint of Reed Books Ltd
Michelin House, 81 Fulham Road, London SW3 6RB
and Auckland, Melbourne, Singapore and Toronto

Copyright in the selection © 1995 by Patrick Garland
Preface copyright © 1995 by the Duke of Richmond and Gordon
Introduction copyright © 1995 by Patrick Garland

A CIP catalogue record for this book is available from the British Library

ISBN 1 85619 725 5

Typeset by Deltatype Ltd, Ellesmere Port, Cheshire
Printed and bound in Great Britain by
Cox & Wyman Ltd, Reading, Berks

Acknowledgements

Acknowledgement is made to the following authors and publishers or their representatives for their permission to use copyright material. Every reasonable effort has been made to clear the use of material in this volume with copyright owners.

Gerald Duckworth and Co. Ltd. and Peters, Fraser and Dunlop for the estate of Hilaire Belloc

Mrs Claire Blunden and A. D. Peters for the poems of Edmund Blunden

Mr Bob Copper

Faber & Faber Ltd for Keith Douglas (1966)

Jonathan Cape (1994) for Vicki Feaver

The Oxford University Press for Christopher Fry

Heinemann Educational Books Ltd. for Robert Gittings

Ensign Publications, Southampton for Tony Wales

Countryside Books, Newbury for Lillian Candlin

Weald and Downland Open Air Museum for Phoebe Somers

Sinclair-Stevenson Ltd (1993) for Nicki Jackowska

Faber & Faber Ltd for Philip Larkin (1964)

Seven Books for Leslie Norris

Faber & Faber Ltd for Ezra Pound

Jonathan Cape (1969) for Ted Walker

Bishop Otter College and Richard Williamson

Chatto and Windus/The Hogarth Press Ltd (1984) for Virginia Woolf

Rupert Hart-Davis for Andrew Young

William Blackwood and Sons Ltd. for Alfred Noyes

The Editor wishes to thank Mr Christopher Fry for his erudite assistance in contributing literary anecdotes; Mr Edward Thomas for painstaking research in attributing Sussex poems by his uncle, Edward Thomas; and Jeannie Brooke Barnett in typing and proof-reading the greater part of this anthology.

You came, and look'd and loved the view
   Long-known and loved by me,
Green Sussex fading into blue
   With one gray glimpse of sea.

ALFRED LORD TENNYSON

Contents

xi

Preface
By the Duke of Richmond and Gordon

In 1737 a porter handed to the Second Duke of Richmond a long poem about Charlton and its Fox Hunt of which the Duke was Master. It included the lines:

> A vast high mountain to the south does bear
> The name of one Saint Roke unknown elsewhere
> A Roman or a Saxon Camp is traced
> On its High Summit . . .

Well, the Trundle, overlooking Goodwood Racecourse, is 676 feet high. St Roke is St Roche (still little known) and the 'Camp' is now known to be pre-Roman.

As a member of a family which has lived for eleven generations at Goodwood in Sussex I am conscious that most people who now live here are 'Incomers' – they came to settle in the county from elsewhere. I have long wanted to help them to understand more of what it means to be a Man or Woman of Sussex.

There is, too, in Sussex, a long history of working men acting and singing. Some plays in part go back as far as Pagan times. I remember 'The Boxgrove Tipteerers' performing their Christmas Mummers' play in verse with violin accompaniment entitled 'St George and the Turkish Knight'. They were mostly estate workers and rehearsed their plays in the 'dinner hour'.

I recollect attending a performance in Goodwood House. The story told of the noble Captain 'Just lately come from France', who boasts what he would do with St George if he were there. St George obligingly comes in, there is an argument and a sword fight. They are parted by the Prince of Peace, who makes his only appearance with the words:

> In come I, the Prince of Peace
> For at this time all blood and warfare
> Now must cease.

The Third Duke, a magistrate, had to try William Blake for sedition in Chichester. Blake was, happily, found 'Not Guilty' and went on to write the words of 'Jerusalem' in the Earl of March pub in Lavant looking towards the Trundle. A century or so later Parry composed the hymn tune for 'Jerusalem' in Rustington, where, decades later Michael Flanders wrote 'The Gnu'!

Hilaire Belloc wrote of desolate 'Ha'nacker Mill' which Stubbs painted in his great canvas *The Charlton Hunt* – still in Goodwood House. The mill still exists because my father formed a trust with others to repair it.

One summer day in 1994, after a fine lunch in good company, I said to Chichester artist David Goodman, 'You know, David, if we had a really good book about Sussex poets, *that* would help give the incomers a feel for Sussex history and people.' Sitting next to Christopher Fry, David said 'I know just the man – Patrick Garland.' And so this book was conceived.

Patrick and David have exceeded my expectations. I am deeply grateful to them as will future generations both of 'Incomers' and native born be grateful to them.

Richmond.

Introduction

In a literary tribute from Japanese writers, after his death in 1974, Tomoji Abe had this to say about Edmund Blunden: 'He is known by everyone to be one of the most English of English poets, and at the same time he could feel with the Japanese. When one loves one's own land well and goes down to its deepest roots one inevitably meets the hearts of mankind. There is no contradiction in it.'

To a certain extent, this would be my personal view of the best of these diverse Sussex poets. There is no contradiction in their disparity. They come from several centuries, and are distinguished by countless differences of temperament, taste, and technique. Some are born in Sussex and explore other places – some are born elsewhere, and explore Sussex. Some from West Sussex, some from East Sussex, as distinctive as continents. So many of the poets, like the inhabitants of the county today, arrive (as do Californians in America) from another state beyond London, discover they like the place, and settle for the rest of their lives. There are those happiest looking out to sea, there are those most reposeful in the Weald, or perched among the uplands; their neighbours far below would not exchange Pevensey or the Manhood Peninsula for Blackdown or the Devil's Punchbowl; some cannot be persuaded to abandon the raffish ambiance of Brighton Pier, others stick fast to their strongholds in Saxon valleys about Burwash and Brimfast; so many, surprisingly find freedom and inspiration at Worthing and Bognor, in particular radical modernists. Lawrence sees the ghosts of World War One dead tumbling out of the white surf on the beach at Bognor Rocks; James Joyce, in the summer of 1923, works on his original drafts of *Finnegan's Wake* in rooms at Clarence Road, in the same sleepy seaside town. He takes the name of one of his principal characters, Earwicker, from a Chichester canon. The explorer of Patagonia, W. H. Hudson, and the naturalist he so admired, Richard Jefferies, end their days in Goring-by-Sea, and lie together in the same churchyard, at Broadwater Cemetery. In his life, Jefferies was familiarly known as 'the Prose Poet of England's fields and woodlands'. It is understandable that Oscar Wilde found the inspiration for Lord Goring and John Worthing among the beach-huts and bathing-machines, but now everybody regrets that the substantial Edwardian set he rented in the autumn of 1894, at 5 The Esplanade, was torn down in favour of an urban block of flats. They would have been a tourist attraction, like the rooms he died in, in the Rue des Beaux-Arts, Paris; these days a fashionable hotel. Most astonishing of all is the invaluable creative partnership in Stone Cottage, Coleman's Hatch, on the isolated boundary of Ashdown Forest: Yeats and Pound, the two foremost pioneers of twentieth-century poetry, meeting, collaborating, even marrying their wives there. Nor were they merely summer holiday visitors, as, it must be confessed, several of the other Sussex writers were. The three years at Stone Cottage, with the fiery, youthful American, Ezra Pound, happily acting as secretary to the older-by-twenty-years William Butler Yeats, proved to be dynamic and revolutionary, with both of them engaged on much of their most innovative and deeply committed poetry. Perhaps what Kipling valued so highly, in his selection of a place to work as well as a place to live, the 'feng shui' – which the Chinese regard as 'the spirit of the place' – proved to be more auspicious in Sussex than elsewhere. Certainly Rudyard Kipling found in the valley below Burwash an imaginary landscape of 'Englishness' which suited his taste, and his quest for 'the Land', and its ancient, primeval, inhabitants. Pook's Hill, with woods above the meadows, is just beyond Batemans. These same 'feng shui' worked less well, alas, for Shelley, who shook the dust of his birthplace, near Horsham, off his feet; also William Blake, who, after a honeymoon period in Sussex of three years, it is felt returned to London in 1803 with a certain degree of relief. Referring in a letter to his erstwhile patron and host, William Hayley, after deserting Felpham for South Molton Street, the visionary genius explains: 'My wife continues poorly, but fancies she is better in health here than by the seaside.' Once again, it was Bognor that provided the fateful lure. George V was less than fair in his imprecation against it, while staying at Aldwick Bay.

In a sense, it is best acknowledged that there is no such thing as 'a Sussex Poet'; that is, in the particular meaning and confinement of the phrase, implying an artist of the majesty of Hardy of Wessex, Brontë of Yorkshire, Constable of Suffolk, Van Gogh of Provence. Nor even, taking the comparison one stage lower, a writer of sufficient stature, that the sense of poetry is forever bound up with the sense of place; as in the example of John Clare in Northamptonshire, or, perhaps better still, A. E. Housman and Shropshire. Hilaire Belloc is passionately the prophet of Sussex, striding its hills, extolling its uplands, singing its songs, and downing its rebarbative beers, *but* he is passionately French for as much of the time, and he writes as robustly about mythical Gallic histories as he does about Downland and Dyke. Andrew Young, the meticulous observer of wildlife and hedgerow, spent many years in Sussex, perhaps his happiest, but he was a minister of the Church of Scotland before he was canon of the Church of England, and his education at Edinburgh informs much of his poetic vision. In technical terms, as prosodist, it should be remembered the Scots have a noble and ancient tradition of writing nature poetry, which reaches back to the fifteenth century. Their first King James of Scotland did not shrink from the composition of exquisite nature poetry himself. As John Betjeman correctly points out, Andrew Young is capable of conveying the atmosphere and scenery of Yorkshire, Wiltshire, Scotland, Kent, Sussex or East Anglia, according to his mood. And therein lies its strength and universality. Perhaps, without wishing to do so consciously, I am returning to the observation made by the Japanese poet, Tomoji Abe, about Edmund Blunden. The more Sussex in spirit, the more English, the more universal, the more, as it were, Japanese. At the risk of sounding a pretentious note, there is no doubt at all that much of Andrew Young's shorter poetry has the precision, the economy of that most admired of Japanese art-forms, the haiku. Belloc brings his elegant French influence to bear, technically, in ballade, villanelle, and tarantelle; Kipling writes of stranded Roman centurions in an altered Britain, and expresses passionately the ancient rhythms of kinship and land, but all the time we hear the footfall of his lost legions on the North-West Frontier, his superb evocation – never improved upon – of 'blunt, bow-headed, whale-backed Downs' as easily brings to life the jungle, the plains, the cities of the night, the bazaars, the speechless veldt. Kipling lived in, and loved Sussex, beyond doubt, but he cannot be claimed as 'one of ours'. The literary map of his planet is greater than Sussex, and he paints, in his own admission 'a four-league canvas, with brushes of comets' hair'. Equally, outsiders, or, as Sussex men would have it, 'furriners', like Keats and Philip Larkin, can visit for a few days, and be inspired to write, in both their cases, among their most-anthologised poems; each, be it said, nourished by similiar monuments in Chichester Cathedral.

This same Gothic monument, dedicated to the Holy and Undivided Trinity, has the distinction, curiously, of being the only English cathedral that can be seen from the sea. In the early years of the century, when visited by Henry James, who lived at the other end of the county, ninety miles away from the Mother-church, in Rye, he complained that the building had only a kind of 'restricted grandeur'; perhaps, with modesty, other than Keats' 'Ode', King's 'Exequy', Larkin's reflections, and Kipling's exhortation, the greater grandeur eludes the county's poets, in a way that in Yorkshire, and Dorset, it does not. If Sussex, however, is not the birthplace of a solitary towering man or woman of genius (and can it be said that Shakespeare contributes much to Warwickshire, other than its economy?), the truth is, both on the surface, and beneath it – I speak in terms of popularity and sheer pleasure – there is a magnificent treasury of Sussex literature, sometimes familiar and cherished, at others, underrated and ignored. Edmund Blunden, Andrew Young, Keith Douglas, W. E. Henley, and Henry King all fall into this overlooked category. For my own taste, not necessarily shared by anybody else, Henry King's 'The Exequy', the lament for his beloved wife's early death, 'To his Matchlesse never to be forgotten Freind', remains undisputably the finest expression of love and regret in the anthology, but it seldom finds its place elsewhere. And Bishop Henry of Chichester scarcely refers in his poems to the city or the county in which he lived successfully so many years; it does not diminish his stature as a Sussex poet.

Perhaps William Blake, of all the singing-birds, as Dr Johnson calls them, was the most distinguished visitor, and his praise (even if finally it turned sour) is eminently worth remembering. It is also the most optimistic: 'Sussex is certainly a happy place,' he wrote, 'and Felpham in particular is the sweetest spot on earth.' He lived in a cottage between 1800 and 1803, which exists today almost as it was when William and Catherine were the occupants. 'Felpham is a sweet place for Study, because it is more Spiritual than London. Heaven opens here on all sides her Golden Gates, voices of Celestial inhabitants are more distinctly heard, their forms more distinctly seen.' Blake continues to delineate the scene from his little cottage, as it was then, surrounded by a flint wall, with cornfields stretching all the way down to the sea. It is as if he speaks from within a painting by his devoted friend, Samuel Palmer:

> Work will go on with God speed. – A roller and two harrows lie before my window. I met a plow on my first going out at my gate the first morning after my arrival, and the Plowboy said to the Plowman, 'Father, the Gate is Open.'

There cannot be a more expressive way to introduce the contents of this anthology – the Gate opens of its own accord to celebrate a season of Sussex Poets.

Patrick Garland
Chichester, June 1995

Bell Chimes in Sussex

An old woman limping,
Says the bells of Clymping,
Bread and cheese on a board,
Says the bells of Ford,
Come in and welcome,
Says the bells of Felpham,
Hurry up or you'll be late,
Says the bells of Faygate,
I'll give you a slap on the pate
Says the bells of Eastergate,
There's more rogues than honest men,
Says the bells of Warbleton,
Shut the gate and clap'n,
Says the bells of Yapton,
Business finished, work begun,
Says the bells of Alfriston.

Hilaire Belloc
(1870–1953)

Belloc 1910

It is good to begin with Hilaire Belloc, as he is closest to the idea of a Sussex poet laureate, passionately identified with the landscape and legend of the county wherein he lives. Sussex was always his home, although he was born in France, of a French mother, and travelled extensively. He first came to Slindon, spent his boyhood in that friendly edge of the South Downs, not far from Arundel, whose River Arun irrigates a valley of sacred water. From an early age he discovered the thrill of prodigious walks (shared with Edward Thomas and Richard Jefferies) and once set out from Petersfield to tramp all the way to Beachy Head, five days' rough hiking, sleeping in the open air, a version of the South Downs Way. Looking back at this time, he remembered: 'In this place, when I was a boy, I pushed through a fringe of beeches that made a complete screen between me and the world, and I came to a glade called No Man's Land. I climbed beyond it, and I was surprised and glad, because from the ridge of that glade I saw the sea.' During his lifetime of eighty-three years, the last ones spent in quietness and virtual senility, Belloc wrote about one hundred and fifty different books, from poetry to travel, histories (he wrote *James II* in just over a week), novels, essays although probably his reputation principally rests on the celebrated 'Cautionary Tales'.

He moved with his family in 1906 to Kings Land, a fourteenth-century village shop, illuminated by candle and oil-lamp, in the village of Shipley, near Horsham, purchased for one thousand pounds, and lived there for the rest of his life. Rumbustious, eccentric in behaviour and dress, something of a professional 'character', he easily attracted a loyal circle of friends, who drank Old Ale and sang Sussex songs, some of which he composed himself. The best of this kind of writing can be found in 'The Four Men', described by Belloc as 'a farrago', which details a hefty ramble around Sussex by four distinctive 'characters', a Poet, a Sailor, 'Myself', and a disenchanted older man, known as Grizzlebeard. They are all, needless to say, versions of the poet, and the journey they make, somewhat drunk and Falstaffian in mood, ends on All Saints' Day, the November Day of the Dead. His final reflections, in the grove above Lavington, have a magical quality, eerily pagan, as he looks north to the rivers and roofs of the Weald. Ignorant of the correct form of benediction with which to bless them:

> I repeated instead the list of their names to serve in place of a prayer:
> ... Amberley Wild brook, which is lonely with reeds at evening; and Burton Great House, where I had spent nights in November; and Lavington, and Hidden Byworth; and Fittleworth next on, and Egdean Side, all heath and air; and the lake and the pine trees, at the Mill; and Petworth, little town. All the land which is knit in with our flesh, and yet in which man cannot find an acre nor a wall of his own.

His life appeared rich and fulfilled, he drank deeply, and cheerfully, was fortified by religious faith as stout as his constitution, and an extensive family. Outwardly, he was assumed to be happy, but the events of his life were not. His wife, Elodie, died young, in 1914, when he was merely forty-four: the loss devastated him for the remainder of his life, and he locked her room, with her possessions within, never to be re-opened, and never failed to cross himself whenever he passed the door. Following that time, he always dressed in black. His eldest son was killed in the First World War, missing in August 1918, in the Royal Flying Corps. His son's bedroom, like Elodie's, was locked for Belloc's lifetime. 'Vision is lost for the moment,' he wrote. 'He is undoubtedly safe, and his mother has him, but the mind in this world has no relief.' In 1941 his other son, Peter, died of pneumonia, when he was in the Royal Marines, and the year following, Belloc suffered a small stroke. He recovered, but was half himself.

Can it be surprising then that beneath the exterior which the outside world thought of as bluff, hearty, optimistic, the deep sense of inward sadness pierces many of the robust rhythms and cheery beats of some of the verses we consider as comic. A. N. Wilson, his sympathetic biographer, points out with some authority that this melancholy strain was always there, and poems like 'Ha'nacker Mill', a particularly striking example of Belloc at his finest, only reiterate that his sense of desolation and elegy was inborn. His epigram, 'The False Heart', speaks perhaps for him, an epitaph not so much for his death, but his life. There was ever something of the Ribstone Pippin about him. But he shall always speak for Sussex:

> He does not die that can bequeath,
> Some influence to the land he knows;
>
>   *   *   *
>
> He does not die but still remains
> Substantiate with his darling plains.

Perhaps this should be thought of as the National Anthem of Sussex, with music by Edward Elgar, when he lived in the woods at Fittleworth.

from The Four Men
The Southern Hills and the South Sea

> The Southern Hills and the South Sea
> They blow such gladness into me,
> That when I get to Burton Sands
> And smell the smell of the Home Lands,
> My heart is all renewed and fills
> With the Southern Sea and the South Hills.

from The Four Men

In the beginning . . .

For when Adam set out (with the help of Eve) to name all the places of the earth (and that is why he had to live so long), he desired to distinguish Sussex, late his happy seat, by some special mark which should pick it out from all the other places of the earth, its inferiors and vassals. So that when Paradise might be regained and the hopeless generation of men permitted to pass the Flaming Sword and to see once more the four

4

rivers, Arun and Adur, and Cuckmere and Ouse, they might know their native place again and mark it for Paradise.

Sonnets

I

Lift up your hearts in Gumber, laugh the Weald
And you my mother the Valley of Arun sing.
Here am I homeward from my wandering,
Here am I homeward and my heart is healed.
You my companions whom the World has tired
Come out to greet me. I have found a face
More beautiful than Gardens; more desired
Than boys in exile love their native place.

Lift up your hearts in Gumber, laugh the Weald
And you my mother the Valley of Arun sing.
Here am I homeward from my wandering,
Here am I homeward and my heart is healed.
If I was thirsty, I have heard a spring.
If I was dusty, I have found a field.

The Roman Catholic Belloc must not be overlooked. One of the Norbetine monks at White Canons, Storrington, frequently celebrated Mass in the family chapel at Kings Land, the same order of monks who befriended Francis Thompson in 1889.

Courtesy

Of Courtesy, it is much less
Than Courage of Heart or Holiness,
Yet in my Walks it seems to me
That the Grace of God is in Courtesy.

On Monks I did in Storrington fall,
They took me straight into their Hall;
I saw Three Pictures on a wall,
And Courtesy was in them all.

The first the Annunciation;
The second the Visitation;
The third the Consolation,
Of God that was Our Lady's Son.

The first was of Saint Gabriel;
On Wings a-flame from Heaven he fell;
And as he went upon one knee
He shone with Heavenly Courtesy.

Our Lady out of Nazareth rode –
It was Her month of heavy load;
Yet was Her face both great and kind,
For Courtesy was in Her Mind.

The third it was our Little Lord,
Whom all the Kings in arms adored;
He was so small you could not see
His large intent of Courtesy.

Our Lord, that was Our Lady's Son,
Go bless you, People, one by one;
My Rhyme is written, my work is done.

The Poet in 'The Four Men' describes this as 'a sort of dirge',
but it is characteristic of the charm Belloc could exert, and by its
close, the delicacy.

6

A Threnody for the Departing Year

Attend, my gentle brethren of the Weald,
Whom now the frozen field
Does with his caking shell your labour spurn,
And turn your shares and turn
Your cattle homeward to their lazy byres;
Oh! gather round our fires
And point a stave or scald a cleanly churn
The while
With ritual strict and nice observance near,
We weave in decent rhyme
A Threnody for the Departing Year.

And you that since the weary world began,
Subject and dear to man,
Have made a living noise about our homes,
You cows and geese and pigs and sheep and all the crew
Of mice and coneys too
And hares and all that ever lurks and roams
From Harting all the way to Bodiam bend,
Attend!
It is a solemn time,
And we assembled here
Advance in honourable rhyme
With ritual strict and nice observance near
Our Threnody for the Departing Year.

The year shall pass, and yet again the year
Shall on our reeds return
The tufted reeds to hurrying Arun dear . . .

As I was passing up your landing towns
I heard how in the South a goddess lay . . .

She ends our little cycle with a pall:
The winter snow shall reverently fall
On our beloved lands

As on Marana dead a winding sheet
Was laid to hide the smallness of her hands,
And her lips virginal:
Her virginal white feet.

I am not sure whether Edward Thomas took his title for his
book of essays on Southern England from Belloc's poem, but
this, together with Kipling's more celebrated 'Sussex', qualifies
as the country's best loved hymn.

The South Country

When I am living in the Midlands
    That are sodden and unkind,
I light my lamp in the evening:
    My work is left behind;
And the great hills of the South Country
    Come back into my mind.

The great hills of the South Country
    They stand along the sea;
And it's there walking in the high woods
    That I could wish to be,
And the men that were boys when I was a boy
    Walking along with me.

The men that live in North England
    I saw them for a day:
Their hearts are set upon the waste fells,
    Their skies are fast and grey;
From their castle-walls a man may see
    The mountains far away.

The men that live in West England
   They see the Severn strong,
A-rolling on rough water brown
   Light aspen leaves along.
They have the secret of the Rocks,
   And the oldest kind of song.

But the men that live in the South Country
   Are the kindest and most wise,
They get their laughter from the loud surf,
   And the faith in their happy eyes
Comes surely from our Sister the Spring
   When over the sea she flies;
The violets suddenly bloom at her feet,
   She blesses us with surprise.

I never get between the pines
   But I smell the Sussex air;
Nor I never come on a belt of sand
   But my home is there.
And along the sky the line of the Downs
   So noble and so bare.

A lost thing I could never find,
   Nor a broken thing mend:
And I fear I shall be all alone
   When I get towards the end.
Who will there be to comfort me
   Or who will be my friend?

I will gather and carefully make my friends
   Of the men of the Sussex Weald,
They watch the stars from silent folds,
   They stiffly plough the field.
By them and the God of the South Country
   My poor soul shall be healed.

If I ever become a rich man,
    Or if ever I grow to be old,
I will build a house with deep thatch
    To shelter me from the cold,
And there shall the Sussex songs be sung
    And the story of Sussex told.

I will hold my house in the high wood
    Within a walk of the sea,
And the men that were boys when I was a boy
    Shall sit and drink with me.

The familiar boisterous, bar-thumping style shows off Belloc's intuitive sense of rhythm, and high spirits – unfashionable, but still good fun, with its built in melody and internal rhyme.

West Sussex Drinking Song

They sell good Beer at Haslemere
And under Guildford Hill.
At Little Cowfold as I've been told
A beggar may drink his fill:
There is a good brew in Amberley too,
And by the bridge also;
But the swipes they take in at Washington Inn
Is the very best Beer I know.

    With my here it goes, and there it goes,
    All the fun's before us:
    The Tipple's aboard and the night is young,
    The door's ajar and the Barrel is sprung,
    I am singing the best song ever was sung
    And it has a rousing chorus.

If I were what I never can be,
The master or the squire:

If you gave me the hundred from here to the sea
Which is more than I desire:
Then all my crops should be barley and hops,
And did my harvest fail
I'd sell every rood of mine acres I would
For a belly-full of good Ale.

With my here it goes, and there it goes,
All the fun's before us:
The Tipple's aboard and the night is young,
The door's ajar and the Barrel is sprung,
I am singing the best song ever was sung
And it has a rousing chorus.

Twelfth Night

As I was lifting over Down,
A winter's night to Petworth Town,
I came upon a company
Of Travellers who would talk with me.

The riding moon was small and bright,
They cast no shadows in her light:
There was no man for miles a-near.
I would not walk with them for fear.

A star in heaven by Gumber glowed,
An ox across the darkness lowed,
Whereat a burning light there stood
Right in the heart of Gumber Wood.

Across the rime their marching rang,
And in a little while they sang;
They sang a song I used to know,
                    Gloria
In Excelsis Domino.

The frozen way those people trod
It led towards the Mother of God;
Perhaps if I had travelled with them
I might have come to Bethlehem.

from The Four Men

The sky was already of an apple green to the westward, and in
the eastern blue there were stars. There also shone what had not
yet appeared upon that windless day, a few small wintry clouds,
neat the defined in heaven. Above them the moon, past her first
quarter but not yet full, was no longer pale, but began to make a
cold glory; and all that valley of Adur was a great and solemn
sight to see as we went forward upon our adventure that led
nowhere and away. To us four men, no one of whom could
know the other, and who had met by I could not tell what
chance, and would part very soon for ever, these things were
given. All four of us together received the sacrament of that
wide and silent beauty and we ourselves went in silence to
receive it.

Ha'nacker Mill

Sally is gone that was so kindly,
Sally is gone from Ha'nacker Hill.
And the Briar grows ever since then so blindly
    And ever since then the clapper is still,
    And the sweeps have fallen from Ha'nacker Mill.

Ha'nacker Hill is in Desolation:
    Ruin a-top and a field unploughed.
And Spirits that call on a fallen nation,
    Spirits that loved her calling aloud:
    Spirits abroad in a windy cloud.

Spirits that call and no one answers;
   Ha'nacker's down and England's done.
Wind and Thistle for pipe and dancers
   And never a ploughman under the Sun.
Never a ploughman. Never a one.

This splendid outburst of bad manners in a theatre is reminiscent of the time Philip Larkin spent an agonising evening at the Oxford Playhouse watching *Playboy of the Western World*. ' "Was I enjoying myself?" I asked. "No, I've never seen such unutterable balls in all my life," and I walked out of the theatre and never came back.' Hilaire Belloc's version is a little more polite.

The World's a Stage

The world's a stage. The trifling entrance fee
Is paid (by proxy) to the registrar.
The Orchestra is very loud and free
But plays no music in particular.
They do not print a programme, that I know.
The cast is large. There isn't any plot.
The acting of the piece is far below
The very worst of modernistic rot.

The only part about it I enjoy
Is what was called in English the Foyay.
There will I stand apart awhile and toy
With thought, and set my cigarette alight;
And then – without returning to the play –
On with my coat and out into the night.

This selection of his Epigrams is concluded by what must surely pass for Hilaire Belloc's epitaph. He died, as he had wished, at

Kings Land, and some of his rooms remain exactly as they used
to be: his grave is at the Catholic church at West Grinstead.

On His Books

When I am dead, I hope it may be said:
'His sins were scarlet, but his books were read.'

Epitaph on the Politician Himself

Here richly, with ridiculous display,
The Politician's corpse was laid away.
While all of his acquaintance sneered and slanged
I wept: for I had longed to see him hanged.

Fatigue

I'm tired of Love: I'm still more tired of Rhyme.
But Money gives me pleasure all the time.

On a Sundial

In soft deluding lies let fools delight.
A Shadow marks our days; which end in Night.

On Another

How slow the Shadow creeps: but when 'tis past
How fast the Shadows fall. How fast! How fast!

Duncton Hill

He does not die that can bequeath
Some influence to the land he knows.
Or dares, persistent, interwreath
Love permanent with the wild hedgerows:
    He does not die, but still remains
    Substantiate with his darling plains.

The spring's superb adventure calls
His dust athwart the woods to flame;
His boundary river's secret falls
Perpetuate and repeat his name.
    He rides his loud October sky:
    He does not die. He does not die.

The beeches know the accustomed head
Which loved them, and a peopled air
Beneath their benediction spread
Comforts the silence everywhere;
    For native ghosts return and these
    Perfect the mystery in the trees.

So, therefore, though myself be crosst
The shuddering of that dreadful day
When friend and fire and home are lost
And even children drawn away –
    The passer-by shall hear me still,
    A boy that sings on Duncton Hill.

William Blake
(1757–1827)

William Blake

The glory of Felpham is that William Blake was happy there for nearly three years. It was at Felpham that he saw the fairy's funeral. 'Did you ever see a fairy's funeral, ma'am?' he asked a visitor. 'Never, sir!' 'I have! ... I was walking alone in my garden; there was great stillness among the branches and flowers, and more than common sweetness in the air; I heard a low and pleasant sound, and I knew not whence it came. At last I saw a procession of creatures, of the size and colour of green and grey grasshoppers, bearing a body laid out on a rose-leaf, which they buried with songs, and then disappeared. It was a fairy's funeral!'

In some verses which Blake addressed to Anna Flaxman, the wife of the sculptor, in September 1800, a few days before moving from London to the Sussex coast, he says:

> Away to sweet Felpham, for Heaven is there;
> The ladder of Angels descends through the air,
> On the turret its spiral does softly descend,
> Through the village then winds, at my cot it does end.

Blake's house still stands, a retired, thatched cottage, facing the sea, but some distance from it.

Samuel Palmer said of his old friend, Blake, whom he knew when he walked the fields around a more modest, and pastoral, London that 'to walk with him in the Country was to perceive the soul of beauty through the forms of matter'.

from Auguries of Innocence

> To see a World in a Grain of Sand
> And a Heaven in a Wild Flower,
> Hold Infinity in the palm of your hand
> And Eternity in an hour.

The villagers of Felpham are not meer Rustics; they are polite and modest. Meat is cheaper than in London, but the sweet air and the voices of winds, trees and birds, and the odours of the happy ground, makes it a dwelling for immortals. Work will go on here with God speed. – A roller and two harrows lie before my window. I met a plow on my first going out at my gate the first morning after my arrival, and the Plowboy said to the Plowman, 'Father, the Gate is Open.'

This was composed by Blake early on in his stay at Felpham, and gives some idea of the pastoral view of the sea from his cottage in 1800 – alas, no more, as it is obscured by holiday homes and the cornfields before the beach, long built over.

First Vision of Light

To my Friend Butts I write
My first Vision of Light,
On the yellow sands sitting.
The sun was Emitting
His Glorious beams
From Heaven's high Streams.
Over Sea, over Land
My Eyes did Expand
Into regions of air
Away from all Care,
Into regions of fire
Remote from Desire;
The Light of the Morning
Heaven's Mountains adorning:
In particles bright

The jewels of Light
Distinct shone & Clear.
Amaz'd & in fear
I each particle gazed,
Astonish'd, Amazed;
For each was a Man
Human-formed. Swift I ran,
For they beckon'd to me
Remote by the Sea,
Saying: Each grain of Sand,
Every Stone on the Land,
Each rock & each hill,
Each fountain & rill,
Each herb & each tree,
Mountain, hill, earth & sea,
Cloud, Meteor & Star,
Are Men Seen Afar.
I stood in the Streams
Of Heaven's bright beams,
And Saw Felpham sweet
Beneath my bright feet
In soft Female charms;
And in her fair arms
My Shadow I knew
And my wife's shadow too,
And My Sister & Friend.
We like Infants descend
In our Shadows on Earth,
Like a weak mortal birth.
My Eyes more & more
Like a Sea without shore
Continue Expanding,
The Heavens commanding,
Till the Jewels of Light,
Heavenly Men beaming bright,
Appear'd as One Man
Who Complacent began
My limbs to infold
In his beams of bright gold;

Like dross purg'd away
All my mire & my clay.
Soft consum'd in delight
In his bosom Sun bright
I remain'd. Soft he smil'd,
And I heard his voice Mild
Saying: This is My Fold,
O thou Ram horn'd with gold,
Who awakest from Sleep
On the Sides of the Deep.
On the Mountains around
The roarings resound
Of the lion & wolf,
The loud Sea & deep gulf.
These are guards of My Fold,
O thou Ram horn'd with gold!
And the voice faded mild.
I remain'd as a Child;
All I ever had known
Before me bright Shone.
I saw you & your wife
By the fountains of Life.
Such the Vision to me
Appear'd on the Sea.

Blake's friend John Flaxman created the marble monument
dedicated to William Collins in the south-west tower of
Chichester Cathedral. William Hayley inscribed the verses.

To Mrs Anna Flaxman

This song to the flower of Flaxman's joy;
To the blossom of hope, for a sweet decoy;
Do all that you can, or all that you may,
To entice him to Felpham and far away.

Away to sweet Felpham, for heaven is there;
The ladder of angels descends through the air;
On the turret its spiral does softly descend,
Through the village then winds, at my cot it does end.

You stand in the village and look up to heaven;
The precious stones glitter on flight seventy-seven;
And my brother is there; and my friend and thine
Descend and ascend with the bread and the wine.

The bread of sweet thought and the wine of delight
Feed the village of Felpham by day and by night;
And at his own door the bless'd Hermit does stand,
Dispensing unceasing to all the wide land.

The 'dark Satanic Mills', so beloved of Women's Institute combined choirs and enthusiasts at the Last Night of the Proms, have nothing to do with the ravages of the industrial revolution, but refer to the oppression he felt from Felpham Mill (and others like it), seven storeys high, just beyond his cottage. It was destroyed some years later, and the foundations have long disappeared under the sea.

from Milton
To Justify the Ways of God to Man

Preface

And did those feet in ancient time
Walk upon England's mountains green?
And was the holy Lamb of God
On England's pleasant pastures seen?

And did the Countenance Divine
Shine forth upon our clouded hills?
And was Jerusalem builded here
Among these dark Satanic Mills?

Bring me my Bow of burning gold:
Bring me my Arrows of desire:
Bring me my Spear: O clouds unfold!
Bring me my Chariot of fire.

I will not cease from Mental Fight,
Nor shall my Sword sleep in my hand
Till we have built Jerusalem
In England's green & pleasant Land.

'Would to God that all the Lord's people were Prophets.'
Numbers, xi. ch., 29 V.

Edward Thomas writes convincingly that although Blake's
bulls 'harnessed with starry harness' are magnificent, they are
nothing to do with Sussex oxen. There is still a case to be made
that the authentic pastoral landscape influenced these lines
from the epic poem Blake was working on during his years at
Felpham. Either way, they are eloquent and little known;
especially the heavenly description of the Nightingale and the
Lark, in stanza 34.

from Milton
Book the First

29

Timbrels & violins sport round the Wine-presses; the little
  Seed,
The sportive Root, the Earth-worm, the gold Beetle, the wise
  Emmet

Dance round the Wine-presses of Luvah: the Centipede is there,
The ground Spider with many eyes, the Mole clothed in velvet,
The ambitious Spider in his sullen web, the lucky golden
 Spinner,
The Earwig arm'd, the tender Maggot, emblem of immortality,
The Flea, Louse, Bug, the Tape-Worm, all the Armies of
 Disease,
Visible or invisible to the slothful vegetating Man.
The slow Slug, the Grasshopper that sings & laughs & drinks:
Winter comes, he folds his slender bones without a murmur.
The cruel Scorpion is there, the Gnat, Wasp, Hornet & the
 Honey Bee,
The Toad & venomous Newt, the Serpent cloth'd in gems &
 gold.
They throw off their gorgeous raiment: they rejoice with loud
 jubilee
Around the Wine-presses of Luvah, naked & drunk with wine.

There is the Nettle that stings with soft down, and there
The indignant Thistle whose bitterness is bred in his milk,
Who feeds on contempt of his neighbour: there all the idle
 Weeds
That creep around the obscure places shew their various limbs
Naked in all their beauty dancing round the Wine-presses.

from Milton
Book the Second

34

Thou hearest the Nightingale begin the Song of Spring.
The Lark sitting upon his earthy bed, just as the morn
Appears, listens silent; then springing from the waving
 Cornfield, loud

He leads the Choir of Day: trill, trill, trill, trill,
Mounting upon the wings of light into the Great Expanse,
Reechoing against the lovely blue & shining heavenly Shell,
His little throat labours with inspiration; every feather
On throat & breast & wings vibrates with the effluence Divine.
All Nature listens silent to him, & the awful Sun
Stands still upon the Mountain looking on this little Bird
With eyes of soft humility & wonder, love & awe.
Then loud from their green covert all the Birds begin their Song:
The Thrush, the Linnet & the Goldfinch, Robin & the Wren
Awake the Sun from his sweet reverie upon the Mountain.
The Nightingale again assays his song, & thro' the day
And thro' the night warbles luxuriant, every Bird of Song
Attending his loud harmony with admiration & love.

*   *   *

First, e'er the morning breaks, joy opens in the flowery bosoms,
Joy even to tears, which the Sun rising dries; first the Wild
    Thyme
And Meadow-sweet, downy & soft waving among the reeds,
Light springing on the air, lead the sweet Dance: they wake
The Honeysuckle sleeping on the Oak; the flaunting beauty
Revels along upon the wind; the White-thorn, lovely May,
Opens her many lovely eyes; listening the Rose still sleeps,
None dare to wake her; soon she bursts her crimson curtain'd
    bed
And comes forth in the majesty of beauty; every Flower,
The Pink, the Jessamine, the Wall-flower, the Carnation,
The Jonquil, the mild Lilly opes her heavens; every Tree
And Flower & Herb soon fill the air with an innumerable
    Dance,
Yet all in order sweet & lovely. Men are sick with Love.

In the months of disenchantment, Blake professed 'the Visions
were angry with me at Felpham'. Imagining Hayley's patronage interfered with his intuitive expression, the poet's resentment came out in these Epigrams. Later, he generously
regretted the violence of his sentiments.

4

Was I angry with Hayley who us'd me so ill,
Or can I be angry with Felpham's old Mill?

6

The Sussex Men are Noted Fools,
And weak is their brain pan:
I wonder if H— the painter
Is not a Sussex Man?

38

TO H—

Thy Friendship oft has made my heart to ake:
Do be my Enemy for Friendship's sake.

43

My title as a Genius thus is prov'd:
Not Prais'd by Hayley nor by Flaxman lov'd

81

23 May, 1810, found the Word Golden.

25

The Angel that presided o'er my birth
Said, 'Little creature, form'd of Joy & Mirth,
Go love without the help of any Thing on Earth.'

Although the relationship with his patron, William Hayley, ended unhappily (he said he was 'determined to be no longer pestered with his genteel ignorance, and polite disapprobation'), Blake had profited from his three years of true pastoral experience and expressed his affection for local people who regretted William and Kate Blake's departure, and showed them many kindnesses.

A Vision of Light

I stood in the Streams
Of Heaven's bright beams,
And Saw Felpham sweet
Beneath my bright feet

I remain'd as a Child;
All I ever had known
Before me bright Shone.

Edmund Blunden
(1896–1974)

The young Edmund Blunden, born in Kent, was educated at Christ's Hospital, the famous Bluecoat School which moved from its original buildings near St Paul's Cathedral in 1902, to an attractive corner of the Bysshe Shelley estate, to the west of Horsham. He was an attentive and successful scholar and intuitive cricketer, and he succeeded well enough at school to be awarded the Senior Grecian Exhibition for Classics in July 1915. A characteristic gesture he made was to recommend in his will, before enlisting into the Sussex Regiment, that his Exhibition at Christ's Hospital should be bequeathed to a less favoured schoolboy, should he, Edmund, be killed in action. While at the Bluecoat School, familiar sights to him were oxen ploughing a wedge of the Downs, familiar smells, fresh churned butter, familiar sounds, the sheer bedlam of nightingales, loud enough to prevent him from sleeping. When Blunden joined up, he belonged to a local Southdown battalion and spoke of it as a family, like some of the northern companies, the 'Acrington Pals', and others. When an unlucky shell exploded their billet at Fleurbaix, the casualties were not chance acquaintances, but five local hearts and heads, intimate with one another as brothers. These experiences of the Western Front, and others as agonising and nightmarish, were to provide the naked material for one of the finest biographies of the battlegrounds in Flanders, *Undertones of War*. In 'The Veteran', an old man trying to forget the war in the tranquillity and reconciliation of his garden, reminds the reader of the old white-haired Elizabethan beadsman, whose 'helmet now a hive for bees becomes . . .'. His frayed dreams of bugles blowing give way to waking to the benevolent sound of a cockerel crowing. In his enthusiastic cricketing days, young Edmund bowled out Ranjitsinjhi in the nets at Brighton, and went on to watch cricket matches at county level at Chichester, but his true love was village cricket. Once he went into bat at number eleven, and kept his end up while the rustic Victor Trumper scored a hundred runs. This hero was Fred Latter, whose life ended tragically short, and he is the white-flannelled shade for whom Blunden wrote the moving tribute to a village cricketer, 'Pride of the Village'.

The Waggoner

The old waggon drudges through the miry lane
  By the skulking pond where the pollards frown,
Notched, dumb, surly images of pain;
  On a dulled earth the night droops down.

Wincing to slow and wistful airs
  The leaves on the shrubbed oaks know their hour,
And the unknown wandering spoiler bares
  The thorned black hedge of a mournful shower.

Small bodies fluster in the dead brown wrack
  As the stumbling shaft-horse jingles past,
And the waggoner flicks his whip a crack:
  The odd light flares on shadows vast

Over the lodges and oasts and byres
  Of the darkened farm; the moment hangs wan
As though nature flagged and all desires.
  But in the dim court the ghost is gone

From the hug-secret yew to the penthouse wall,
  And stooping there seems to listen to
The waggoner leading the gray to stall,
  As centuries past itself would do.

The Unchangeable

Though I within these two last years of grace
  Have seen bright Ancre scourged to brackish mire,
And meagre Belgian becks by dale and chace
  Stamped into sloughs of death with battering fire, –
Spite of all this, I sing you high and low,

My old loves, waters, be you shoal or deep,
Waters whose lazy and continual flow
Learns at the drizzling weir the tongue of sleep.

For Sussex cries from primrose lags and brakes,
'Why do you leave my woods untrod so long?
Still float the bronze carp on my lilied lakes,
Still the wood-fairies round my spring wells throng;
And chancing lights on willowy waterbreaks
Dance to the dabbling brooks' midsummer song.'

The Estrangement

Dim through cloud veils the moonlight trembles down,
A cold grey vapour, on the huddling town;
And far from cut-throat's corner the eye sees
Unsilvered hogs'-backs, pallid stubble leas;
Barn-ridges gaunt and gleamless: blue like ghosts
The knoll mill and the odd cowls of the oasts,
And lonely homes pondering with joys and fears
The dusty travail of three hundred years.

In the ashen twilight momently afield,
Like thistle-wool wafting across the Weald,
Flickers the sighing spirit; as he passes,
The lispering aspens and the scarfed brook grasses
With wakened melancholy writhe the air.

In the false moonlight wails my old despair,
And I am but a pipe for its wild moan;
Crying through the misty bypaths; slumber-banned;
Impelled and voiced, to piercing coronach blown:

A hounded kern in this grim No Man's Land,
I am spurned between the secret countersigns
Of every little grain of rustling sand

In these parched lanes where the gray wind maligns;
Oaks, once my friends, with ugly murmurings
Madden me, and ivy whirs like condor wings:
The very bat that stoops and whips askance
Shrills malice at the soul grown strange in France.

The Veteran

For G. H. Harrison

He stumbles silver-haired among his bees,
Now with the warm sun mantling him; he plods,
Taking his honey under the pippin-trees,
Where every sprig with rich red harvest nods.
    He marks the skies' intents,
And like a child, his joy still springing new,
In this fantastic garden the year through
He steeps himself in nature's opulence.

Mellow between the leafy maze smiles down
September's sun, swelling his multitude
Of gold and red and green and russet-brown
Lavished in plenty's lusty-handed mood
    For this old man who goes
Reckoning ripeness, shoring the lolling sprays,
And fruits which early gusts made castaways
From the deep grasses thriftily rescuing those.

Babble he will, lingeringly, lovingly,
Of all the glories of this fruitful place,
Counting the virtues of each several tree,
Her years, her yield, her hardihood or grace;
    While through this triumph-song,
As through their shielding leaves, the year's fruits burn
In bright eye-cozening colour, turn by turn,
From cool black cherries till gold quinces throng

Blossoming the blue mists with their queenly scent . . .
Who hearing him can think what dragging years,
Of drouthy raids and frontier-fights he spent,
With drum and fife to drown his clamouring fears? . . .
    Here where the grapes turn red
On the red walls, and honey in the hives
Is like drift snow, contentment only thrives,
And the long misery of the Line is dead.

Resting in his old oaken-raftered room,
He sits and watches the departing light
Crimsoning like his apple-trees in bloom,
With dreaming gratitude and calm delight.
    And fast the peering sun
Has lit the blue delft ranged along the wall,
The painted clock and Squirrel's Funeral,
And through the cobwebs traced his rusty gun.

And then the dusk, and sleep, and while he sleeps,
Apple-scent floods and honey's fragrance there,
And old-time wines, whose secret he still keeps,
Are beautiful upon the marvelling air.
    And if sleep seem unsound,
And set old bugles pealing through the dark,
Waked on the instant, he but wakes to hark
His bellman cockerel crying the first round.

Forefathers

Here they went with smock and crook,
    Toiled in the sun, lolled in the shade,
Here they mudded out the brook
    And here their hatchet cleared the glade:
Harvest-supper woke their wit,
Huntsman's moon their wooings lit.

From this church they led their brides,
    From this church themselves were led
Shoulder-high; on these waysides
    Sat to take their beer and bread.
Names are gone – what men they were
These their cottages declare.

Names are vanished, save the few
    In the old brown Bible scrawled;
These were men of pith and thew,
    Whom the city never called;
Scarce could read or hold a quill,
Built the barn, the forge, the mill.

On the green they watched their sons
    Playing till too dark to see,
As their fathers watched them once,
    As my father once watched me;
While the bat and beetle flew
On the warm air webbed with dew.

Unrecorded, unrenowned,
    Men from whom my ways begin,
Here I know you by your ground
    But I know you not within –
There is silence, there survives
Not a moment of your lives.

Like the bee that now is blown
    Honey-heavy on my hand,
From his toppling tansy-throne
    In the green tempestuous land –
I'm in clover now, nor know
Who made honey long ago.

Wilfrid Blunt
(1840–1922)

In spite of his exotic appearance (he rode around his vast estate in flowing Arab robes) Wilfrid Blunt considered himself far closer to Sussex soil than either Kipling or Belloc, whom he thought of as upstart 'incomers', not *born* in the county as he was. When Ezra Pound and Yeats came over from Stone Cottage, Coleman's Hatch, to pay their respects to the old poet, he offered them roast peacock. Originally, Wilfrid Scawen Blunt inherited a lavish 2,000 acre estate, Crabbett Park at Worth, and moved later to Southwater, near Horsham. He wrote these lines on 'A Day in Sussex' there, and also 'Chanclebury Ring'.

A Day in Sussex

The dove did lend me wings. I fled away
From the loud world which long had troubled me.
Oh lightly did I flee when hoyden May
Threw her wild mantle on the hawthorn-tree.
I left the dusty high-road, and my way
Was through deep meadows, shut with copses fair.
A choir of thrushes poured its roundelay
From every hedge and every thicket there.
Mild, moon-faced kine looked on, where in the grass
All heaped with flowers I lay, from noon till eve.
And hares unwitting close to me did pass,
And still the birds sang, and I could not grieve.
Oh what a blessed thing that evening was!
Peace, music, twilight, all that could deceive
A soul to joy or lull a heart to peace.
It glimmers yet across whole years like these.

Wilfrid Blunt invented one couplet almost – but not quite – as expressive as Tennyson's 'View from Blackdown Forest':

> On this side in its glory lay the sea,
> On that the Sussex Weald, a sea of brown.

Chanclebury Ring

Say what you will, – there is not in the world
A nobler sight than from this upper down.
No rugged landscape here, no beauty hurled
From its Creator's hand as with a frown;
But a green plain on which green hills look down
Trim as a garden plot. No other hue
Can hence be seen, save here and there the brown
Of a square fallow, and the horizon's blue.
Dear checker-work of woods, the Sussex weald.
If a name thrills me yet of things of earth,
That name is thine! How often have I fled
To thy deep hedgerows and embraced each field,
Each lag, each pasture, – fields which gave me birth
And saw my youth, and which must hold me dead.

Not dissimilar to Wilfrid Blunt's sentiments, these lines of Mrs Browning express the deep feeling experienced by the true devotees of the South Downlands – a form of yearning, like a sailor for the sea, which is found in the words and writings of the nomadic shepherds of the old days.

Elizabeth Barrett Browning

My own hills! Are you 'ware of me my hills
How I burn toward you? Do you feel to-night
The urgency and yearning of my soul
As sleeping mothers feel the sucking babe
And smile? . . . Still ye go
Your own determined, calm, indifferent way
Toward sunrise, shade by shade, and light by light.

Thomas Campbell
(1777–1844)

Lines on the Camp Hill Near Hastings

In the deep blue of Eve,
Ere the twinkling of stars had begun,
  Or the lark took his leave
Of the skies and the sweet setting sun,
  I climbed to yon heights
Where the Norman encamped him of old,
  With his bowmen and knights,
And his banner all burnish'd with gold . . . .
  Over hauberk and helm
As the sun's setting splendour was thrown,
  Thence they look'd o'er a realm –
And to-morrow beheld it their own.

William Collins
(1721–1759)

William Collins is unique insofar as he was born, lived, was educated, died and was buried in Chichester. His father was the celebrated hatter 'Collins of Chichester'. His birthplace in East Street, Chichester, is now offices of a building society. William Hayley wrote his inscription upon a marble memorial tablet in the Cathedral of exquisite design by Blake's friend, John Flaxman. His most celebrated lines are:

> How sleep the Brave, who sink to Rest
> By all their Country's Wishes blest!

from his 'Ode, written in the beginning of the Year, 1746'. There is something sympathetic and forlorn about him, although he had a reputation for indolence and dissipation. After his death in Chichester in 1759, Gilbert White of Selborne wrote, under a pseudonym, a warm-hearted letter to the *Gentleman's Magazine* extolling the young man's qualities and humility. 'He was of a moderate stature, of a light and clear complexion, with grey eyes, so very weak at times, as hardly to bear a candle in the room, often raising with him apprehensions of blindness.' Even more eloquently, Dr Johnson spoke of his somewhat tragic temperament in *Lives of the Poets*. He knew him relatively well, at the time Collins came to London in 1744, with ambitions to be a historian or a playwright, and with customary precision, said of him, 'he planned several tragedies, but he only planned them. Probably not a page was ever written.' A poignant failure then, and yet he has his place in our literature, and nobly on one of the walls of Chichester Cathedral. 'Such was the fate of Collins,' writes the kindly Doctor, 'with whom I once delighted to converse, and whom I yet remember with tenderness.' Poor Collins wrote little which is coherent or notable after the age of twenty-five – he suffered from an imprecise mixture of melancholia, inebriation and insanity, his friends regretted his imperceptible decline, which in my view was what we call familiarly Alzheimer's disease. To have composed such delicate classical Odes, and to be remembered by Dr Johnson, with tenderness, is, all the same, a notable achievement.

Ode to Pity

O Thou, the Friend of Man assign'd,
With balmy Hands his Wounds to bind,
    And charm his frantic Woe:
When first *Distress* with Dagger keen
Broke forth to waste his destin'd Scene,
    His wild unsated Foe!

2

By *Pella's* Bard, a magic Name,
By all the Grief's his Thought could frame,
    Receive my humble Rite:
Long, *Pity*, let the Nations view
Thy sky-worn Robes of tend'rest Blue,
    And Eyes of dewy Light!

3

But wherefore need I wander wide
To old *Ilissus'* distant Side,
    Deserted Stream, and mute?
Wild *Arun** too has heard thy Strains,
And Echo, 'midst my native Plains,
    Been sooth'd by *Pity's* Lute.

4

There first the Wren thy Myrtles shed
On gentlest *Otway's* infant Head,
    To Him thy Cell was shown;

* The River *Arun* runs by the Village in *Sussex*, where *Otway* had his Birth.

And while He sung the Female Heart,
With Youth's soft Notes unspoil'd by Art,
   Thy Turtles mix'd their own.

5

Come, *Pity*, come, by Fancy's Aid,
Ev'n now my Thoughts, relenting Maid,
   Thy Temple's Pride design:
Its Southern Site, its Truth compleat
Shall raise a wild Enthusiast Heat,
   In all who view the Shrine.

6

There Picture's Toils shall well relate,
How Chance, or hard involving Fate,
   O'er mortal Bliss prevail:
The Buskin'd Muse shall near her stand,
And sighing prompt her tender Hand,
   With each disastrous Tale.

7

There let me oft, retir'd by Day,
In Dreams of Passion melt away,
   Allow'd with thee to dwell:
There waste the mournful Lamp of Night,
Till, Virgin, Thou again delight
   To hear a *British* Shell!

Ode

Written in the beginning of the Year 1746

How sleep the Brave, who sink to Rest,
By all their Country's Wishes blest!
When *Spring*, with dewy Fingers cold,
Returns to deck their hallow'd Mold,

She there shall dress a sweeter Sod,
Than *Fancy's* Feet have ever trod.

2

By Fairy Hands their Knell is rung,
By Forms unseen their Dirge is sung;
There *Honour* comes, a Pilgrim grey,
To bless the Turf that wraps their Clay,
And *Freedom* shall a-while repair,
To dwell a weeping Hermit there!

Charles Crocker
(1797–1861)

Collins' Monument

In Chichester Cathedral

Now sleeps the Bard in peace, who through life's day
    Of rest and peace, alas! but little knew;
Disease, and pain, and care, in grim array,
    Ever around his path their shadows threw;
And sick at heart, and weary, he withdrew,
    Hopeless – alike unstrung his lyre and mind,
    And sought in shades remote, like wounded hind,
To hide his sufferings deep from mortal view.
    But as the Dove of old flew far and wide,
And found no rest, save in the Ark alone,
    E'en so the Poet back returned – his guide
Truth's holy light – that ark of refuge shone
    Bright in the beams of Faith and Hope, and bore
    His spirit free and glad, to Rest's untroubled shore.

William Congreve
(1670–1729)

The Sussex men that dwell upon the shore
Look out when storms arise and billows roar,
Devoutly praying with uplifted hands,
That some well-laden ships may strike the sands,
To whose rich cargo they may make pretence,
And fatten on the spoils of Providence.

Bob Copper
(1915–   )

Bob Copper, the great Sussex patriot, who celebrated his eightieth birthday this year, has kept alive the real tradition of authentic folk-songs, poems, and rural dialect. He is the grandfather and grandson of true Rottingdean countrymen.

Bob left school at fourteen and worked as lather-boy in the local barber's shop in his village. Today he is a folk-singer of national reputation. If it can be true of anybody, it is true of Bob Copper that in *his* home, as Belloc writes:

> There shall the Sussex songs be sung,
> And the story of Sussex told.

He and his sons can sing not only of drinking, but of the ale-barrels, and the Sussex inns where the ale was drunk, and those who do the drinking.

Me and My Little Barrel

> O good drop of beer, I love thee
> In thee I put my trust
> I'd sooner bed with a belly-full
> Than go to bed with a thirst.
> Good drop of beer I love thee
> You robs me of all my clothes,
> But good drop of beer I love thee,
> So down my throat you goes.

This is one of Bob Copper's traditional folk-songs of a more robust nature. Here is a classic illustration of what is meant when the reader imagines he can *hear* the tune it goes to, even if he doesn't know it. 'My Old Man' has the ring of authenticity. The song also possesses an almost Chaucerian timelessness, and narrative strength, genuine wit, and a convincing case for guileful Sussex womanhood.

My Old Man

My old man come home last night, come home last night did he,
Straightway into the stable and a strange horse there he'd see.
'Whose horse is this, whose horse is that, whose ever can it be?'
'Oh don't you know it's a milking cow that grandma sent to me.'
　'Miles have I travelled, ten thousand miles or more,
　But a milking cow with harness on I never have seen before.'

Now my old man come home last night, come home last night did he,
Straightway into the boot-room and a strange pair of boots he'd see.
'Whose boots are these, whose boots are they, whose ever can they be?'
'Oh don't you know they're milking pails that grandma sent to me.'
　'Miles have I travelled, ten thousand miles or more,
　But milking pails with laces I never have seen before.'

Now my old man come home last night, come home last night did he,
Straightway into the cloakroom and a strange coat there he'd see.
'Whose coat be this, whose coat be that, whose ever can it be?'
'Oh don't you know it's a blanket, dear, that grandma sent to me.'
　'Miles have I travelled, ten thousand miles or more,
　But a blanket with brass buttons on I never have seen before.'

45

Now my old man come home last night, come home last night
    did he,
Straightway into the bedroom and a strange face there he'd see.
'Whose face is this, whose face is that, whose ever can it be?'
'Oh don't you know it's a baby, dear, that grandma sent to me.'
    'Miles have I travelled, ten thousand miles or more,
    But a baby's face with whiskers on I never have seen before.'

Phoebe Somers

from A Time There Was

Life Was Sweet

Some of these old farm workers were not averse to a bit of history, as I found when chatting one day with an old shepherd near the Saxon church at Sompting. 'That were done in the war,' said George Humphries, pointing to some ruins nearby. I expressed some surprise and said that I didn't know that the Germans had bombed Sompting. He gave me a long, hard look as he replied, 'It were Cromwell and his lot!'

The rough hard lives of these people seem to have left them ungrudging, though difficulties and discomforts are readily admitted. They sum up their working days in crisp, short sentences which have the ring of truth: 'The work was pretty tough but it didn't do us no harm.' 'They were happy days in spite of the difficulties.' 'I've had a rough and tough working life, but a happy one.'

The word 'happy' is constantly used when they speak of the past and this may well be due to the fact that they were satisfied to work along with their peers and their animals.

An 87-year-old woodman, Albert Roberts who, incidentally, was proud of having lived through six reigns and had spent all his life in the Sussex woodland, summed it up in three simple words: 'Life was sweet,' he said.

The Old Field Routine

Out in the morning at four o'clock. Mouthful of bread and cheese and pint of ale. Then off to the harvest field. Rippin and moen (reaping and mowing) till eight. Then morning brakfast and small beer. Brakfast – a piece of fat pork as thick as your hat (a broad-brimmed wideawake) is wide. Then work till ten o'clock: then a mouthful of bread and cheese and a pint of strong beer ('farnooner', i.e. forenooner: 'farnooner's-lunch', we called it). Work till twelve. Then at dinner in the farmhouse; sometimes a leg of mutton, sometimes a piece of ham and plum pudding. Then work till five, then a 'nunch' and a quart of ale. Lunch was cheese, 'twas skimmed cheese though. Then work till sunset, then home and have supper and a pint of ale. I never knew a man drunk in the harvest field in my life. Could drink six quarts, and believe that a man might drink two gallons in a day.

When the hay was in cock or the wheat in shock, then the Titheman come; you didn't dare take up a field without you let him know. If the Titheman didn't come at the time, you tithed yourself. He marked his sheaves with a bough or bush. You couldn't get over the Titheman. All the tithing was quiet. You didn't dare even set your eggs till the Titheman had been and ta'en his tithe.

R. Thurston Hopkins

The Devout Life

Shepherds were allowed to bring their dogs into church up to 1800 – and it may be guessed that the dogs occasionally indulged in a general *mêlée*.

Interesting as a specimen of pastoral folk-lore was the burial custom of sending a dead shepherd on his final journey with an emblem of his calling clutched in his hand. The custom has now become obsolete, but I remember one of the Collins family at Hooe, near Bexhill, telling me that he remembered seeing a shepherd buried with a sheepskin for a winding sheet, but this seems to be a unique instance in Sussex. However, during the Great War many of our men were hurriedly buried in their sheepskin jerkins. The old custom was to put a lock of wool into the shepherd's hand, the idea being that on Judgment Day he could display the symbol of his vocation in order to show why he was so frequently absent during divine service.

Bob Copper

This is a poem Bob Copper wrote himself, which refers to this ancient tradition.

A Shepherd's Prayer

On a summer Sunday evening
For a brief half hour of ease,
Ben, the shepherd, sits and ponders
While the sun shines through the trees,
And the honey bees buzz softly
As they blunder to and fro'
From the purple-spotted foxgloves
To the white hives in a row.

Here his garden is untended
And the nettles grow waist high;
In the ash tree zephyrs whisper
Softer than a maiden's sigh.
Down the path he looks with pleasure
At the runner beans grown tall,
And the ripening tomatoes
Up against the churchyard wall.

Sees the rows of peas and carrots
And the rosemary and sage,
All laid out with neat precision
Like the printing on a page.
Sees he, too, the jackdaw perching
On the steeple weather-vane.
Hears the laughter of the children
Playing hop-scotch down the lane.

Now the week has turned full circle
And the wheels have ceased to spin,
Opens he his heart to heaven
And lets peace come drifting in.
All is well and life is moving
On its due appointed course
Following in blind obedience
To some hallowed, unknown force.

CLANG! The bells crash from the belfrey
And his thoughts are all undone,
Flying like a flock of starlings
When they hear the keeper's gun.
Then from cottage, hall or farm or
Other places where they dwell,
Come the faithful, trotting briskly
To the summons of the bell.

Meeting at the ancient lych-gate,
Greeting with a nod and smile,
On their Sunday-best behaviour,
Dressed in best but sober style.
Clutching in their hands their prayer-books,
Hurrying e'er the hymn begins,
Clutching, also, in their hearts
Their little weekly crop of sins.

Grocermen who give short measure
Mixing sugar up with sand,
Men who climb another's staircase
While he's working on the land.
Practicers of greed and gossip
Here for absolution seek
To emerge, the service over,
Blameless for another week.

Some attend from merely habit,
Some are on the Church guild list,
Others only make appearance
Lest their presence might be missed.

In the church 'twas dark and gloomy
And the air was dank and chill.
Outside in a blaze of fire the
Sun went down behind the hill.
Ben gazed up in silent wonder
At the green gold afterglow,
Watched with awe a single star
Shed twinkling light on earth below.

'I en't, Lord, had no truck with church –
Shepherds dun't have time t'go.
They used t' put a lock o' wool
Inside their coffins so You'd know.
I likes t' watch the sky be night
An' see how bright that star do shine,
But, if church be the only road,
Here's one, O Lord, as wun't be gwine.'

R. Thurston Hopkins

Sheep-Bell Music

There is nothing quite like the Sussex sheep-bells anywhere else in the world, and their music rarefied by the silence and innumerable hollows and slopes of the Downs would lose its mellow charm in other surroundings. The lover of the Downs will feel the riddle of the sheep-bells, and their drowsy klonk-klonk-klonk – a muffled golden sound – will wrack his heart with some emotion of which God keeps the secret . . . some old thing which eternally floats between joy and sorrow. Why should a sheep-bell be common-place? Why should it be grotesque to say that its tune is sweeter than that of a harp or a violin? The music of our sheep-bells is full of beauty, and whoever is touched by their drowsy lullaby takes a magic from outside the world.

Charles Crocker
(1797–1861)

The Chichester Shoemaker, Charles Crocker, joins John Clare, the Northamptonshire Peasant Poet, Robert 'Ploughboy' Burns, Robert 'Farmer's Boy' Bloomfield, Stephen Duck and James Taylor, 'the Water Poet', as examples of the patronage of the Rural Muse – sons of the soil, taken up for a short time, and, all too frequently, rejected, by the nobility and intelligentsia.

Charles Crocker began, apprenticed to a cobbler, from humble beginnings, worked his way up until he graduated to be a local bookseller, and Sexton of the Cathedral at Chichester. He ended his days as Bishop's Verger, which were, he said, the happiest of his life; this was rather unlike the other 'peasant poets'.

Kingley Vale is a secretive grove of ancient yew-trees, somewhat sinister on winter evenings, claimed by a few to be the burial-ground of Danish Kings.

Verses from Kingley Vale

How beautiful, embosom'd in the hill
And cloth'd in sunshine, the sweet dell appears,
As summer noontide bright, as midnight still;
There on its sloping side, where, full of years,
Stands the dark yew, the slender ash uprears
Its silver shaft – while with the holly's shade,
In beauteous contrast that the sight aye cheers,
The oak and beech, in varied tints array'd,
Their boughs luxuriant twine as if they ne'er would fade.

Who does not feel in solitude like this,
A holy freedom from the shackles base

Of cares and passions that destroy the bliss
Of life mid busy haunts, or in the chase
Of fortune's gifts, or in the wild embrace
Of sensual pleasure? Here the soul is free
To commune with the Genius of the place;
To bow at Nature's shrine, and glow, till we
Anticipate the joys of immortality.

*   *   *

Above the rest, amid the smiling vale,
Cicesteria's Fane pre-eminent appears,
A sight that in my mind can never fail
To wake sweet thoughts of home and other years.
'Twas there the voice of Truth first charm'd mine ears,
And bade me hope for bliss beyond the tomb:
And this it is that to my heart endears
That sacred Pile – in sunlight or in gloom
I gaze upon its walls, and think of heav'n and home.

There was a time, ere yet Refinement's hand
Had brought from distant climes her glittering store,
When this now richly-cultivated land
Was one vast desert; forest, heath, and moor,
In savage wildness stretch'd from shore to shore.
Brief is the record History's page contains
Of times so far remote: Tradition's lore
Hath much reveal'd; and on our hills and plains
Of those rude ages yet full many a trace remains.

Mid such e'en now I stand. Tradition says
Beneath these very hillocks Sea-kings sleep, –
Those fierce marauders who, in Alfred's days,
From Scandinavia, with destructive sweep,
Launch'd forth to reign despotic on the deep,
And fill with woe and death each neighbouring shore.
While here I muse, reclin'd on this green heap,
Fancy shall wing her flight to days of yore,
And to enrich my theme Oblivion's shades explore.

This poem proved to be disastrously prophetic, when, following prolonged rains in the winter of 1994, the Downs saturated the spring source at East Dean and the tributary of the Lavant turned into a ferocious torrent, reclaiming its former, built-over course. 'Black Ruin', as the Chichester Shoemaker warned, virtually 'followed quite'.

The Lavant

I've seen thy waters with a torrent's force
Restless and with loud and rushing sound
Dash forward in their wild impetuous course,
As if they scorned thy channel's narrow bound;
While Winter on the naked landscape frowned
In sullen majesty, and with a blast terrific,
Call'd his gathering storms around:
Black Ruin followed quite, where'er they passed
And o'er creation's force thick gloom and horror cast.

The River Lavant

Amidst the South Saxonian hills,
there runs a verdant fruitful Vale, in
which, at once fower small,
and pretty Villages are seen;
Eastden the one, does first supply the
spring,
whence milky Lavant, takes his future
course; Charleton, the next, the beauty of
the fower,

from twenty chalky rills, fresh vigour
adds,
then swiftly on, his force redoubled,
he thro' all the meads, to Singletown does
glide;
more Strength, he there receives,
at Westden next, his last recruit he
makes,
then boldly runs, till lefs confin'd,
he wider spreads his Fame,
and passing Lavant, there he takes his
Name.
He then begins, to do what good he can,
during his Short live'd, Transitory reign:
here mills for corn, demand his present
aid,
there Farmers beg! his virtue he'll im-
part,
t'inrich their lands, for greater future
crops.
Requests all granted, to the Ocean,
he as proudly marches,
as the greatest of all the confed'rate
Rivers of the Land . . .

From the records of the Old Charlton Hunt written anony-
mously in 1737.

The pub at Charlton, a typical downland village, used to carry
the charming name of The Fox Goes Free. One of the most
memorable hunts in eighteenth-century English rural history
was the Chase which began at Charlton, where the Duke of
Richmond kept his stables, and legendary pack of foxhounds.
   The description is entirely factual, but it reads like a most

elaborate piece of poetry, a veritable litany of time-honoured warrens, furzes and coppices. I observe an early use of the verb 'blew', meaning 'muffed'.

An epitaph to the huntsman, Tom Johnson, follows, who took part in this remarkable chase with Nim Ives and Cornet Honywood, as whippers-in. The final couplet is worthy of the best of John Dryden.

The Remarkable Chase

At a quarter before eight in the morning the fox was found at Eastdean Wood, and ran an hour in that cover; then up into the Forest, up to Puntice Coppice through Heringdean to the Marlows, to the Forest West Gate, over the fields to Nightingale Bottom, to Cobden's at Draught, up his Pine Pit Hanger, where His Grace of St Alban's got a fall; through My Lady Lewknor's Puttocks, and missed the earth; through Westdean Forest to the corner of Collar Down (where Lord Harcourt blew his first horse), crossed the Hackney-place down the length of Coney Coppice, through the Marlows to Heringdean, into the Forest and Puntice Coppice, Eastdean Wood, through the Lower Teglease across by Cocking Course down between Graffham and Woolavington, through Mr Ormes Park and Paddock over the Heath to Fielder's Furzes; to the Harlands, over Todham Heath, almost to Cowdray Park, there turned to the limekiln at the end of Cocking Causeway, through Cocking Park and Furzes; there crossed the road and up the hills between Bepton and Cocking. Here the unfortunate Lord Harcourt's second horse felt the effects of long legs and a sudden steep; the best thing that belonged to him was his saddle, which My Lord had secured; but, by bleeding and Geneva he recovered, and with some difficulty was got home. Here Mr Farquhar's humanity claims your regard, who kindly sympathised with My Lord in his misfortunes, and had not power to go beyond him. At the bottom of Cocking Warren the hounds turned to the left across the road by the barn near Heringdean, then took the side near to the north-gate of the Forest (Here General Hawley thought it prudent to change his horse for a true-blue that staid up the hills). Billy Ives likewise took a horse of Sir Harry Liddell's, went quite through the Forest and run the foil through Nightingale Bottom to Cobden at Draught, up his Pine Pit Hanger to My Lady Lewknor's Puttocks, through every mews she went in the morning; went through the Warren above Westdean (where we dropt Sir Harry Liddell) down to Benderton Farm (here Lord Harry sank), through Goodwood Park (here the Duke of Richmond chose to send three lame horses back to Charlton, and took Saucy Face and Sir William, that were luckily at Goodwood; from thence, at a distance, Lord Harry was seen driving his horse before him to Charlton). The hounds went out at the upper end of the Park over Strettington-road by Sealy Coppice (where His Grace of Richmond got a summerset), through Halnaker Park over Halnaker Hill to Seabeach Farm (here the Master of the Stag Hounds, Cornet Honywood, Tom Johnson, and Nim Ives were thoroughly satisfied), up Long Down, through Eartham Common fields and Kemp's High Wood (here Billy Ives tried his second horse and took Sir William, by which the Duke of St Alban's had no great coat, so returned to Charlton). From Kemp's High Wood the hounds took away through Gunworth Warren, Kemp's Rough Piece, over Slindon Down to Madehurst Parsonage (where Billy came in with them), over Poor Down up to Madehurst, then down to Houghton Forest, where His Grace of Richmond, General Hawley, and Mr Pauncefort came in (the latter to little purpose, for, beyond the Ruel Hill, neither Mr Pauncefort nor his horse Tinker cared to go, so wisely returned to his impatient friends), up the Ruel Hill, left Sherwood on the right hand, crossed Ofham Hill to Southwood, from thence to South Stoke to the wall of Arundel River, where the glorious 23 hounds put an end to the campaign, and killed an old bitch fox, ten minutes before six. Billy Ives, His Grace of Richmond, and General Hawley were the only persons in at the death, to the immortal honour of 17 stone, and at least as many campaigns.

Epitaph to a Huntsman

NEAR THIS PLACE LIES INTERRED
THOMAS JOHNSON,
WHO DEPARTED THIS LIFE AT CHARLTON
DECEMBER 20th, 1744

Here JOHNSON lies – what Hunter can deny
Old, honest TOM the Tribute of a sigh.
Deaf is that Ear, which caught the op'ning Sound;
Dumb is that Tongue, which chear'd the Hills around.
Unpleasing truth – Death hunts us from our Birth
In view; and Men, like Foxes, take to Earth.

On the subject of epitaphs, this, in a country graveyard, is
dignified and restrained in grief, more likely to have been
penned by William Hayley, or William Collins, than the
anonymous country stonemason. The child referred to in these
lines is Meneleb Raynsford, aged nine, who died in 1627.

A Child's Grave

Great Jove hath lost his Gannymede, I know,
Which made him seek another here below –
And finding none – not one – like unto this,
Hath ta'en him hence into eternal bliss.
Cease, then, for thy dear Meneleb to weep,
God's darling was too good for thee to keep:
But rather joy in this great favour given,
A child on earth is made a saint in heaven.

Charles William Dalmon

Interwoven among the Bellocs, Blakes, Keats and Kiplings, I have included work by famous writers, of the stature of, for example, Swinburne, or Galsworthy, who may have only written *one* poem concerning the county – or, of lesser poets who may have written many poems, but from whose output, only one merits consideration.

This eulogy of local poets by Charles Dalmon is affectionate and well-intended, even if lacking in sophistication – E. V. Lucas, whose *Highways and Byways in Sussex* is one of the finest of that splendid series, thought it worthy of inclusion. It is called 'The Sussex Muse', which would make an alternative, albeit predictable, title for this book.

The Sussex Muse

For where the damask roses, mignonette,
Stocks, tiger-lilies, musk, and mint diffuse,
Their night-fresh fragrance, and the moonlight makes
The colours mystical, the Sussex Muse,
Wrapt in a veil of mist, alights and takes
Her Pan-pipes, jewel set,
Out from between her breasts, and, for myself
Alone, against the sundial leans and plays
The very tunes she played in bygone days
To Fletcher, Otway, Collins, Shelley, Realf.

When Shelley's soul was carried through the air,
Toward the manor-house where he was born,
I danced along the avenue at Denne,
And Praised the grace of heaven and the morn,

Which numbered with the sons of Sussex men,
A genius so rare!
So high a honour, and so dear a birth,
That, though the Horsham folk may little care
To laud the favour of his birthplace there,
My name is bless'd for it throughout the earth.

I taught the child to love and dream and sing
Of witch, hobgoblin, folk, and flower lore;
And often led him by the hand away
Into St. Leonard's forest, where of yore
The hermit fought the dragon – to this day,
The children, ev'ry spring,
Find lilies of the valley blowing where
The fights took place. Alas! they quickly drove
My darling from my bosom and my love,
And snatched my crown of laurel from his hair.

Keith Douglas
(1920–1944)

The crucial link between Keith Douglas and Edmund Blunden and Sussex is Christ's Hospital. There was always a poetic tradition at the celebrated Bluecoat School – Charles Lamb, Coleridge, George Peele, and Leigh Hunt were all schoolboys there. Like Edmund Blunden, who cast a favourable eye over pupils with literary talent, Keith Douglas was born in Kent. At school, he quickly earned a reputation for a gifted but angular personality: in later years, people found him aggressive and self-centred on the one hand, sensitive and artistic on the other. It is difficult to imagine a poet's sensibility otherwise. At Christ's Hospital he gained a scholarship. The wonder is how advanced and 'modern' the tone of Keith Douglas's work is, when one thinks he was only a public school teenager when he wrote it. The Georgians were no model for him – he was always a contemporary talent. Christopher Fry, who at that time edited an anthology of schools' poetry, immediately spotted something rare and remarkable and was the first to actually publish him in a magazine.

Edmund Blunden, in 1939 at Merton College (and later his tutor in English Literature), championed the younger poet's cause, and tried to persuade T. S. Eliot to publish him, unsuccessfully. Eliot seldom made errors, and later on, satisfactorily, Faber & Faber published Douglas's poetry, and his explosive journal of the Desert War, *Alamein to Zem Zem*. This was sent to Blunden first, who advised the young tank-officer to temper some of his more alarming views, but admired the violent power and suppressed rage, and in the late, alas, great poems, approved of the irony and premonition of death.

The literary world – when Douglas was killed in action in July 1944, only his third day in Normandy – mourned a poet in the tradition of Wilfred Owen and Siegfried Sassoon; his fellow soldiers only knew they missed a courageous and conscientious officer. But Douglas was more than a war poet: in an altogether too short life, he tried to pack in as much as he could. He disliked rhetoric, and any kind of affectation, and his statement on poetry has an assured place in the Theory of Literature. As Lawrence Durrell wrote of him – his poetry is not the work of a virtuoso, but the early work of a real master – we have every right to regret he ran out of time so quickly.

Mummers

Put by your stitching. Spread the table
With winking cups and wines. That sable
Doff for your brighter silks: are all
Your glints of pearly laughter shuttered?
See where the outdoor snows, wind-fluttered,
Through the arched window fall.

See where the deep night's blast has straddled
The ancient gargoyle, weather-addled
And striped with melted tapestry
Of snow; his evil face well-carven
By Brother Ambrose, lean and starven,
Cell-fasting, rich in artistry.

Soon come the masked mummers, knocking
With hands snow-red. The door's unlocking
Answers the stars with indoor light.
Now to the drum tap, with snow-crusted
Cardboard steed, and ancient rusted
Blade, the Saint and Turk will fight.

Written, presumably at school as a teenager, Keith Douglas's poem about the traditional military rifle-gauge is ominously prophetic of his own battle experience in the North African campaign and in Normandy in 1944.

I have looked through the pine trees
cooling their sunwarmed needles in the night
I saw the moon's face, white,
beautiful as the breeze.

Yet you have seen the trees sway'd with the night's breath
wave like dead arms, repudiating the stars
and the moon, circular and useless pass
pockmarked with death.

Through a machine-gun's sights
I saw men weep, cough, sprawl in their entrails.
You did not know The Gardener in the vales.
Only efficiency delights you.

Love and Gorizia

And now in the South the swallows
Swirling precisely among the dazzled trees
are not known, not at this season, among these
small streets and posters which the lamplight shews:
but are among the white-dusted avenues,
and where the ruined palace faces the green
river, and barbers chatter, the sky is clean.

Mr Kennedy, speaking in Painswick among slate,
insisted on shadows' value, thought
colour of merely secondary import;
characteristically, being himself incomplete,
wound-drained, among these places, where thus late
the unsatisfied put out their heads, take pleasure
in reproducing rooftops on rough paper.

This my comparison of where I found you
with South, redolent of wingtips, suddenly gold,
you small with your red-brown hair how could I mould,
so inconsistent, how could I take you? So renew
desires, Birdlip for Aquileia, different view
forswearing swallows. Spinsters on their stools
more valuable than monks until Desire cools.

On Leaving School

Here where the years stand under us in the valley
We can look down upon their shops and vineyards
And honestly say we would rather be like leopards
Let out in one direction, who cannot be silly.

And at this evening moment, when the shallow
Echoes stagger against Big School, it is awkward
Realizing happiness seems just to have started
And now we must leave it, live like trees or charlock.

One of us will be the kettle past care of tinkers,
Rejected, one the tip-top apple, the winking
Sun's friend. It will be that way, and Time on our ground
Will sweep like a maid, and where we were be clean.
Shall we find room to laugh, if turning round
We see where we have walked, how wrong we have been?

A Statement on Poetry

Oxford 1940

Poetry is like a man, whom thinking you know all his
movements and appearance you will presently come upon in

such a posture that for a moment you can hardly believe it a position of the limbs you know. So thinking you have set bounds to the nature of poetry, you shall as soon discover something outside your bounds which they should evidently contain.

The expression 'bad poetry' is meaningless: critics still use it, forgetting that bad poetry is not poetry at all.

Nor can prose and poetry be compared any more than pictures and pencils: the one is instrument and the other art. Poetry may be written in prose or verse, or spoken extempore.

For it is anything expressed in words, which appeals to the emotions either in presenting an image or picture to move them; or by the music of words affecting them through the senses; or in stating some truth whose eternal quality exacts the same reverence as eternity itself.

In its nature poetry is sincere and simple.

Writing which is poetry must say what the writer has himself to say, not what he has observed others to say with effect, nor what he thinks will impress his hearers because it impressed him hearing it. Nor must he waste any more words over it than a mathematician: every word must work for its keep, in prose, blank verse, or rhyme.

And poetry is to be judged not by what the poet has tried to say; only by what he has said.

A God is Buried

I

Turn your back on Monte Nero, that mountain
to the west. Turn your back on the white town
of Gorizia, plastered with notices and swarming
with soldiers. Cross the green Isonzo. Go down

by the ruined palace of the archbishop, the machine-gun
    schools,
and a company of the Alpini with their mules:
then uphill to where hundreds of saplings hide
where a generation of men and trees died:

and where the bright blood and shrapnel are sunk in grass
the golden oriole fluting in a cool hollow
colours the silence. These musical spirits pass
ahead and to the left. Now if you follow

you will come where high explosive could not move
the god who's buried in this flowering grove,
but he has slept two hundred decades here.

No music will wake his marble. Not yet;
still he must rest in soil and forget
another madness begun this year.

Aristocrats

'I think I am becoming a God'

The noble horse with courage in his eye,
clean in the bone, looks up at a shellburst:
away fly the images of the shires
but he puts the pipe back in his mouth.

Peter was unfortunately killed by an 88;
it took his leg away, he died in the ambulance.
I saw him crawling on the sand, he said
It's most unfair, they've shot my foot off.*

How can I live among this gentle
obsolescent breed of heroes, and not weep?

68

Unicorns, almost,
for they are fading into two legends in which their stupidity
    and chivalry
are celebrated. Each, fool and hero, will be an immortal.

These plains were their cricket pitch
and in the mountains the tremendous drop fences
brought down some of the runners. Here then
under the stones and earth they dispose themselves,
I think with their famous unconcern.
It is not gunfire I hear, but a hunting horn.

* 'Lt. Col. J. D. Player, killed in Tunisia, Enfidaville, Feb. 1943, left £3,000 to the Beaufort hunt, and directed that the incumbent of the living in his gift should be "a man who approves of hunting, shooting, and all manly sports, which are the backbone of the nation".'

Vergissmeinnicht

Three weeks gone and the combatants gone
returning over the nightmare ground
we found the place again, and found
the soldier sprawling in the sun.

The frowning barrel of his gun
overshadowing. As we came on
that day, he hit my tank with one
like the entry of a demon.

Look. Here in the gunpit spoil
the dishonoured picture of his girl
who has put: *Steffi. Vergissmeinnicht*
in a copybook gothic script.

We see him almost with content,
abased, and seeming to have paid

and mocked at by his own equipment
that's hard and good when he's decayed.

But she would weep to see today
how on his skin the swart flies move;
the dust upon the paper eye
and the burst stomach like a cave.

For here the lover and killer are mingled
who had one body and one heart.
And death who had the soldier singled
has done the lover mortal hurt.

Mein Mund ist stumm, aber mein Aug'es spricht
Und was es sagt ist kurz – Vergissmeinnicht.
Steffi

Deliberately mixed up among the classical poets, a part of what follows is a hotch-potch, a miscellany – some lively verse, some doggerel (colloquial prose), and some old Sussex dialect, including local proverbs, epitaphs, old wives tales, and other kinds of country chatter. To me, it is colourful, funny, rich in language, earthy, and to be cherished. It may not be Collins or Keats, but it is unquestionably, deep Sussex. Sussex is wealthy in splendid-sounding words of country dialect – here are a few, whose absence in present day speech is a tragic loss for Poetry.

Old Dialect Words

Lapsy	– forgetful
Taffety	– fastidious
Didicoi	– half-gypsy, or today, a pikey
Tissicky	– tickling sore throat
Poucher	– broad bean
Scroop	– scraping noise
Kitterwise	– at any time
Ampre-Aug	– aching-tooth
Peter-grievous	– a fractious, uncontrollable child

Christopher Fry told me of a gardener he knew who was always grumbling. He was known in the village as Captain Grievous. Dave Ainger bears an ancient Sussex name, often found in eighteenth- or nineteenth-century references, and he worked as gardener for my home in 'The Manhood' long before I lived there. It is a curious, low-lying landscape to the south of Chichester petering out towards the sea, more like Suffolk than traditional downland Sussex. The area is renowned for sunlight, and the fertile growth of vegetables – Mr Ainger told me his father always referred to it as 'God's Little Apron'. The local word for gardens (and sometimes, graveyards) is 'gay-ground'. Both in Kent and Sussex I have noted the professional gardener's term for compost, or manure, is 'the amendment'.

E. V. Lucas
(1868–1938)

Ditchling

The village of Ditchling could not well be more out of the movement, yet an old lady living in the neighbourhood who, when about to visit London for the first time, was asked what she expected to find, replied, 'Well, I can't exactly tell, but I suppose something like the more bustling part of Ditchling.' A kindred story is told of a Sussex man who, finding himself in London for the first time, exclaimed with astonishment – 'What a queer large place! Why, it ain't like Newick and it ain't like Chailey.'

Michael Drayton
(1563–1631)

Belonging firmly to the school of poets who have written about Sussex, but lived somewhere else entirely, Michael Drayton qualifies for inclusion, neither for the merit of his verses, nor for the originality of his theme. But, in writing about 'the Daughters of the Weald', Michael Drayton, the Tudor poet and tragedian, undertakes the examination of what must have been at the time a serious ecological crisis – the genuine equivalent in the Weald of the depredation of the Amazon rain forests. Composed in 1622, Drayton's masterpiece, 'Polyolbion' (a handful of excellent sonnets apart), remains his topographical survey of England. His subject is the collapse of the Sylvan green world of what used to be called 'Wooden England', the era of the Forest of the Andredswald, which separated the southern coastline from the arteries which led to London and York. It is hard to think of them now, but their impenetrable darkness concealed dragons, and giant serpents, sinister native inhabitants, and a ghastly man-sized predator, known as the Bustard, which was powerful enough to haul riders from horseback and devour them. The destruction of the woods had already begun by the middle of the sixteenth century, and Drayton was really witnessing its ultimate death-throw. 'These iron times,' he warns, 'breed none that mind posterity.' A fretful admonition, as deeply felt as Philip Larkin's poem 'Going, Going', when he laments,

> And that will be England gone,
> The shadows, the meadows, the lanes,
> The guildhalls, the carved choirs . . .
> > all that remains
> For us will be concrete and tyres.

The Mayor of Rye complained in 1581 that because of the massive wood-burning to fuel the iron-works, '. . . the woddes growing nere unto the three towns of Hastings, Winchelsey and

Rye, are marvaylously wasted and decayed . . .' Times change, but do not vary. In the later part of the poem, it is to be noted, when the Rivers Arun and Lavant take their watery revenge, 'but braking into rage, wisht Tempests them might rive'. History recollected itself when the local rivers broke their banks in the winter of 1994, and flooded the culverts, threatening the foundations of Chichester Cathedral itself. Local opinion blamed for the near-disaster, rather than the sheer volume of rain on the Downs, the human interference in altering the river-courses for housing development, and denuding the natural banks of tree roots, whose customary thirst succeeded in lowering the water levels.

from Polyolbion

> The daughters of the Weald
> (That in their heavy breasts had long their griefs concealed),
> Foreseeing their decay each hour so fast come on,
> Under the axe's stroke, fetched many a grievous groan.
> When as the anvil's weight, and hammer's dreadful sound,
> Even rent the hollow woods and shook the queachy ground;
> So that the trembling nymphs, oppressed through ghastly fear,
> Ran madding to the downs, with loose dishevelled hair.
> The Sylvans that about the neighouring woods did dwell,
> Both in the tufty frith and in the mossy fell,
> Forsook their gloomy bowers, and wandered far abroad,
> Expelled their quiet seats, and place of their abode,
> When labouring carts they saw to hold their daily trade,
> Where they in summer wont to sport them in the shade.
> 'Could we,' say they, 'suppose that any would us cherish
> Which suffer every day the holiest things to perish?
> Or to our daily want to minister supply?
> These iron times breed none that mind posterity.
> 'Tis but in vain to tell what we before have been,
> Or changes of the world that we in time have seen;
> When, now devising how to spend our wealth with waste,

We to the savage swine let fall our larding mast,
But now, alas! ourselves we have not to sustain,
Nor can our tops suffice to shield our roots from rain.
Jove's oak, the warlike ash, veined elm, the softer beech,
Short hazel, maple plain, light asp, the bending wych,
Tough holly, and smooth birch, must altogether burn;
What should the builder serve, supplies the forger's turn,
When under public good, base private gain takes hold,
And we, poor woeful woods, to ruin lastly sold.'
So did the envious Downes; but that againe the Floods
(Their fountains that derive, from those unpittied Woods,
And so much grace they Downes, as through their Dales they
    creep,
Their glories to convey unto the Celtick deep)
It very hardly tooke, much murmuring at their pride.
Cleere Lauant, that doth keep the Southamptonian side
(Dividing it well-neere from the Sussexian lands
That Selsey doth survay, and Solents troubled sands)
To Chichester their wrongs impatiently doth tell:
And Arun, (which doth name the beautious Arundell)
As on her course she came, it to her Forrest tolde.
Which, nettled with the newes, had not the power to hold:
But breaking into rage, wisht Tempests them might rive;
And on their barren scalps, still flint and chauke might thrive,
The brave and noble Woods which basely thus upbraid.

Fairy Folk

Many Sussex place-names testify to the firmly held belief in the
fairy folk throughout the county – Faygate, Pookbourne, Pook
Hole, Pook-Ryde, Pook Hale, and Puck's Church Parlour, to
name just a few.

Farisees and the Axey

AXEY. The ague. A complaint which is very prevalent in many parts of Sussex. There is a different name for it in almost every district. In some places it is believed that it may be cured by the following charm, which, to be efficacious, must be written on a three-cornered piece of paper and worn round the neck till it drops off:

> Ague, ague, I thee defy,
> Three days shiver,
> Three days shake,
> Make me well for Jesus' sake!

A spider is considered a useful insect for the cure of the ague. If taken internally, it should be rolled up in a cobweb and swallowed like a pill. If applied externally, it should be placed in a nutshell and hung round the neck in a bag of black silk.

Among other Sussex remedies it is said that a mouse roasted alive is good for the whooping-cough.

FARISEES. Fairies. By an unfortunate use of the reduplicated plural, the Sussex country people confuse the ideas of fairies and Pharisees in a most hopeless manner. A belief in fairies is by no means extinct in the South Down districts, and among other stories the following was most seriously told me:

I've heard my feather say, that when he lived over the hill, there was a carter that worked on the farm along wid him, and no one couldn't think how t'was that this here man's horses looked so much better than what any one else's did. I've heard my feather say that they was that fat that they couldn't scarcely get about; and this here carter he was just as much puzzled as what the rest was, so cardinley he laid hisself up in the staable one night, to see if he could find the meaning an't.

And he hadn't been there very long, before these here liddle farisees they crep in at the sink hole; in they crep, one after another; liddle tiny bits of chaps they was, and each an 'em had a liddle sack of corn on his back as much as ever he could carry. Well! in they crep, on they gets, up they clims, and there they was, just as busy feeding these here horses; and prensley one says to t'other, he says, 'Puck,' says he, 'I twets, do you twet?'

(Sweat.) And thereupon, this here carter he jumps up and says, 'Dannel ye,' he says, 'I'll make ye twet afore I've done wud ye!' But afore he could get anigh 'em they was all gone, every one an 'em.

And I've heard my feather say, that from that day forard this here carter's horses fell away, till they got that thin and poor that he couldn't bear to be seen along wid 'em, so he took and went away, for he couldn't abear to see hisself no longer and nobody aint seen him since.

A Sussex man was once asked, 'What is a pharisee?' and answered, with much deliberation and confidence, 'A little creature rather bigger than a squirrel, and not quite so large as a fox,' and I believe he expressed a general opinion.

> If apples bloom in March,
> In vain for them you'll search.
> If apples bloom in April,
> Why then they will be plentiful,
> But if apples bloom in May,
> You may eat 'em night and day.

> The cuckoo comes in April,
> He sings his song in May,
> In the middle of June, he cracks his tune,
> In July he flies away.

The Sussex Devil is familiarly known as 'The Old Man', 'The Poor Man' (curiously) and 'Old Scratch'.

> Ridgick [Rudgwick] for riches,
> Green [Wisborough Green] for poors,
> Billingshurst for pretty girls,
> And Horsham for whores.

Vicki Feaver
(1943–   )

Vicki Feaver is on the permanent teaching staff in the English department of Bishop Otter College, Chichester, and also a force in the innovative creative writing course as a lecturer, and, which is as important, a practitioner. She comes originally from Durham and took her degree in music from that university and later was awarded first class honours in the University of London. Her first book of poems, written in 1981, is called *Close Relatives* and *The Handless Maiden*, her second collection, received excellent reviews when it came out in 1993, more than fulfilling the original promise of her first book. Her poems are unexpectedly fierce and candidly sensuous, reminiscent some of the time of D. H. Lawrence. By contrast she lives in West Ashling, a traditional Sussex village, and images of her life in the region have found their way in to recent poems. A walk along the shingle beach at Church Norton, the presumed site of the original cathedral, long believed lost, inspired 'Horned Poppy', and the chalk Downs produced 'Glow Worm': tricks of light and shadow, surreal cloudscapes, and a toad found in the cellar of her cottage.

Wasps

If you don't hurt them
they won't hurt you,
my father told me.

But I didn't believe him,
or that he wasn't afraid
as he wafted them

wildly away
with shaking,
nail-bitten fingers.

And now the wasps
have invaded again,
building a nest

in the roof-space,
scratching at the eaves
with fierce little jaws,

finding a way into rooms
through closed doors
and windows,

as they did in that other
heat-struck autumn
when we had to lift him

to change the sheets,
or rub surgical spirit
into his heels

and buttocks;
when a dozy wasp
crawled in

under his pyjama top
and clung like a brooch
to his bubbling chest.

Judith

Wondering how a good woman can murder
I enter the tent of Holofernes,
holding in one hand his long oiled hair
and in the other, raised above
his sleeping, wine-flushed face,
his falchion with its unsheathed
curved blade. And I feel a rush
of tenderness, a longing
to put down my weapon, to lie
sheltered and safe in a warrior's
fumy sweat, under the emerald stars
of his purple and gold canopy,
to melt like a sweet on his tongue
to nothing. And I remember the glare
of the barley field; my husband
pushing away the sponge I pressed
to his burning head; the stubble
puncturing my feet as I ran,
flinging myself on a body
that was already cooling
and stiffening; and the nights
when I lay on the roof – my emptiness
like the emptiness of a temple
with the doors kicked in; and the mornings
when I rolled in the ash of the fire
just to be touched and dirtied
by something. And I bring my blade
down on his neck – and it's easy
like slicing through fish.
And I bring it down again,
cleaving the bone.

Lovers

after Andrew Wyeth

At dawn, he shakes her awake
and gets her to sit on a stool
by the open window.
He studies the way a white
low-lying sun fastens long shadows
down the bank behind the house

and enters the dark room, touching
her cheek, neck, straggling braids,
breast, arm, thigh, ankle.

A dead leaf blows over the sill
and she catches it in her hand,
holds it out like a child.

He orders her to be still,
then sketches it in – the shrivelled leaf
against her live skin.

Her nipples are rosy and hard.
He can smell the fox stink of her sex.
He'll paint her a few more times –

but always buttoned up to the neck
in a heavy loden coat,
further and further from the house,

deeper and deeper
into the frozen woods,
as if returning her to the wild.

Rev. A. Frewen Aylward

I have put these verses under F for Frewen, rather than A for Aylward, because they would get us off to an awkward start, compared with Belloc or Blake! This is rather typical poetry of the 'Sussex Wunt be Druv' school. There's a great deal of it, mostly written between 1870 and 1929, and at its best there is a sort of robust, patriotic, earthy, pint-of-beer vigour about it – but it is far removed from Kipling and Belloc, from whom it is said, erroneously in my view, to have derived. It seems best to be rather sparing with the genre, but it has its place. Arthur Beckett and W. Victor Cook are other exponents of the folkloric school of rustic verse, as opposed to Bob Copper and his family, who succeed in keeping in touch with the authentic strain. A good ear can effortlessly tell the difference.

Sussex Folk

I

Some praise the sturdy northland
    Whose sons are tall and strong,
Some make the busy midland
    The burthen of their song:
And east is east, and west is west,
    Each with its separate spell,
But the land for me skirts the southern sea,
    And the praise of its folk I'd tell.
        Clay of the weald, chalk of the down
        Breeze from the boisterous sea,
    These are the things make Sussex men
        The sort of folk they be!

You may see them pull the hop poles,
  You may see them guide the plough,
You may see them launch the lugger
  While the waves break o'er her bow;
And when the war cloud gathered
  And the country called for aid,
Men of the shire – son, brother and sire –
  Stood ready and undismayed!
    Men of the marsh and moorland,
      Sons of the shore or sea,
    Heaven keep you still, through good or ill,
      The sort of folk you be.

III

And if the men of Sussex
  Be brave and strong and true,
Their matrons and their maidens
· Have many a virtue too.
Mothers and wives and sweethearts
  No comelier can be seen,
Than those who grace some lordly place,
  Or reign as village queen!
    Fragrance of flower and hop-bine,
      Beauties of sky and sea,
    Make Sussex maids and matrons,
      The sort of folk they be!

It seems only correct to find out where 'Sussex by the Sea' actually comes from at last.

Although the familiar song of that name, the marching song of The Sussex Regiment, is a little different, and is written by Ward-Cook, Kipling uses the final line to infinitely more dignified effect in his ode to Sussex, which includes the superb phrase 'our blunt, bow-headed, whale-backed Downs'.

This is a rather less-elevated attempt at Kiplingese, and illustrates how removed it is from the real thing. This kind of hearty light verse always contains within it an awkward air of self-congratulation, and appears to have mislaid its tune.

from Song O' the Sussex Men

Saint Wilfrid sailed to Sussex, an' he come to Selsey Bill,
An' there he built a liddle church upon a liddle hill;
He taught the starving pagans how to net fish from the sea,
An' then he them converted all to Christianitee.

CHORUS

For it's good to live in Sussex, the land o' the brave an' free,
Where men are bruff and honest – such men as you an' me;
If you weren't born in Sussex, whoever you may be,
Then come an' *die* in Sussex land, sweet Sussex by the Sea!

Arthur F. Bell

Arthur Bell has come up with a more dignified version; some of the lines are musical, some of the poet's phrases, felicitous.

The Hidden City

I am fain to find God's city
    That lies hid in Sussex hills,
I see its far-off glory
    When the wide-winged sunset fills
The coombes with misty amber,
    And the ruffling day-wind stills.

That glory shrouds no domes or towers
    Of lordly palaces,
But deep-browed thatch and gables wide
    And kindly Sussex trees,
Whose mighty arms hold peace above
    The simple cottages.

I hear its happy murmur
    Sometimes at eve or morn,
When all the air is very still,
    As though the song were borne
Of men knee-deep in falling grass
    Or harvesting the corn.

Footsore and bowed and weary,
    Some day I may creep down
The winding street no angels tread,
    But peasants strong and brown,
And hear their deep-voiced speech, and know
    Myself in God's own town.

To conclude:
The archetypal dialect song, written, surprisingly, not in 1850, but 1950, is meant to summon up a smiling image of stubborn local character. I wonder whether it does.

W. Victor Cook

Sussex Won't Be Druv

Some folks as comes to Sussex,
　They rackons as they knows
A darn sight better what to do
Then silly folks like me and you
　Could possibly suppose.
But them as comes to Sussex,
　They mustn't push and shove,
For Sussex will be Sussex,
　And Sussex won't be druv.

Mus' Wilfrid came to Selsey.
　Us heaved a stone at he,
Because he rackoned he could teach
Our Sussex fishers how to reach
　The fishes in the sea.
But when he dwelt among us,
　Us gave un land and love,
For Sussex will be Sussex,
　And Sussex won't be druv.

All folks as comes to Sussex
　Must follow Sussex ways,
And when they've larned to know us well
There's no place else they'd wish to dwell
　In all their blessed days.
There ant no place like Sussex
　Until you goes Above,
But Sussex will be Sussex
　And Sussex won't be druv.

Christopher Fry
(1907–   )

An extremely youthful 87-year-old, sprightly of mind and foot, and held in great affection by a large circle of good friends, Christopher Fry still lives in the same cottage in East Dean he bought, with his wife, Phyl, when they arrived at the invitation of the poet, Robert Gittings, in the summer of 1967. East Dean, the virtual source of the River Lavant, celebrated in several early poems in this collection, is one of the most enchanting and characteristic of West Sussex downland villages. The little river runs through Chichester to the sea. His play, *Boy with a Cart* (written long before this time, in 1944), already celebrated one of the most-loved Sussex saints, and several of his plays have been produced by the Festival Theatre at Chichester with great success, as well as all over the world. He is still prolific, and generous with his time as well as his gifts, writing graceful, well-tuned lyrics on any number of local occasions – the opening of the Weald and Downland Open Air Museum at Singleton, the twenty-fifth anniversary of the Chichester Festival Theatre, its founder's ninetieth birthday, the celebration of the Chichester Cathedral, the inauguration of an imaginative open-air sculpture museum. He still prefers to work on the old-fashioned Corona typewriter he first used as a young writer, which was manufactured in 1917, and has been his faithful friend since 1932. When he lived in Sussex first, years before East Dean, he and his wife stayed in a Mill in Coleman's Hatch, and it was some time before he learnt that Stone Cottage, where Yeats and Pound lived in the First World War, was only a short stroll away. 'Boy with a Cart' was first performed for the parish church at Coleman's Hatch. Christopher Fry was the English teacher at my first prep-school, Hazelwood, in Limpsfield Chart, on the North Downs, before the war. One of the form-masters at the same time (with general teaching duties, and not exclusively music) was Michael Tippett. Remembering the somewhat philistine education I received there in the 1940s, I cannot help but think a little wistfully of a halcyon age when sixth-form Music and English might have been the responsibility of Mr Tippett and Mr Fry!

The Weald & Downland Open Air Museum, Singleton

Now, when Time has taken
  To hurling itself away
So that the length of a week
  Seems hardly to last a day.

We can recover our breath
  Here, where yester-days
Are brought back to a valley
  Like sheep that safely graze:

A quiet coming together
  Of centuries in one place
Where the long fingers of time
  Can reach and interlace.

Here we can stem for a little
  The flowing years that pass,
And open a door on the distance
  Of a living time that was:

Feel by sun-or-rainlight
  The heretofore,
And see the human shadow
  Crossing the floor.

Hathill Copse, Goodwood

We walk the strange familiar earth
Between the receiving hands of stone
Into a place of shaping-forth
Where trees make sculptures of their own,
And light and shadows and the human hand
Draw music out of silence, setting free
A dance of stillness over a living land
Which reaches to the sea.

When out of sleep we come from sunless dream
We look again on measure and form, the play
Of moving air across the surface of time,
The curve and ceremony of a day
Housing us for a while. Here, as though eyes
Had been given to the blind stone, a vision awoken
Like Adam out of the dust of paradise,
The silence at the world's dark centre is broken.

Coda: As it has always been,
           Making seen the unseen,
           Over centuries before
           Between this woodland and the shore
           The spire of the cathedral stands,
           Nave, treasury and choir,
           The transfiguring of stone by human hands.

Reprise: We walk the strange familiar earth
           Between the receiving hands of stone
           Into a place of shaping-forth
           Where trees make sculptures of their own,
           And light and shadow and the human hand
           Draw music out of silence, setting free
           A dance of stillness over a living land
           Which reaches to the sea.

from The Boy With A Cart

THE PEOPLE OF SOUTH ENGLAND:
In our fields, fallow and burdened, in grass and furrow,
In barn and stable, with scythe, flail, or harrow,
Sheepshearing, milking or mowing, on labour that's older
Than knowledge, with God we work shoulder to shoulder;
God providing, we dividing, sowing, and pruning;
Not knowing yet and yet sometimes discerning:
Discerning a little at Spring when the bud and shoot
With pointing finger show the hand at the root,
With stretching finger point the mood in the sky:
Sky and root in joint action; and the cry
Of the unsteady lamb allying with the brief
Sunlight, with the curled and cautious leaf.

 Coming out from our doorways on April evenings
 When to-morrow's sky is written on the slates
 We have discerned a little, we have learned
 More than the gossip that comes to us over our gates.
 We have seen old men cracking their memories for dry milk.
 We have seen old women dandling shadows;
 But coming out from our doorways, we have felt
 Heaven ride with Spring into the meadows.

We have felt the joint action of root and sky, of man
And God, when day first risks the hills, and when
The darkness hangs the hatchet in the barn
And scrapes the heavy boot against the iron:
In first and last twilight, before wheels have turned
Or after they are still, we have discerned:
Guessed at divinity working above the wind,
Working under our feet; or at the end
Of a furrow, watching the lark dissolve in sun,

We have almost known, a little have known
The work that is with our work, as we have seen
The blackthorn hang where the Milky Way has been:
Flower and star spattering the sky
And the root touched by some divinity.

Coming out from our doorways on October nights
We have seen the sky unfreeze and a star drip
Into the south: experienced alteration
Beyond experience. We have felt the grip
Of the hand on earth and sky in careful coupling
Despite the jibbing, man destroying, denying,
Disputing, or the late frost looting the land
Of green. Despite flood and the lightning's rifle
In root and sky we can discern the hand.

It is there in the story of Cuthman, the working together
Of man and God like root and sky, the son
Of a Cornish shepherd, Cuthman, the boy with a cart,
The boy we saw trudging the sheep-tracks with his mother
Mile upon mile over five counties; one
Fixed purpose biting his heels and lifting his heart.
We saw him; we saw him with a grass in his mouth, chewing
And travelling. We saw him building at last
A church among whortleberries. And you shall see
Now, in this place, the story of his going
And his building. – A thousand years in the past
There was a shepherd, and his son had three
Sorrows come together on him. Shadow
The boy. Follow him now as he runs in the meadow.

(*They set off on their journey, the* MOTHER *in the cart, and a
rope round* CUTHMAN'S *neck attached to the handles. As they
go* CUTHMAN *begins to whistle. They are heard going away into
the distance.*)

THE PEOPLE OF SOUTH ENGLAND:
Stone over stone, over the shaking track,

They start their journey: jarring muscle and aching
Back crunch the fading county into
Dust. Stone over stone, over the trundling
Mile, they stumble and trudge: where the thirsty bramble
Begs at the sleeve, the pot-hole tugs the foot.
Stone over stone, over the trampled sunlight,
Over the flagging day, over the burn
And blister of the dry boot, they flog their way
To where the journeyless and roofless trees
Muster against the plunging of the dark:
Where the shut door and the ministering fire
Have shrunk across the fields to a dog's bark,
To a charred circle in the grass.
No floorboard mouse, no tattling friend; only
The flickering bat dodging the night air,
Only the stoat clapping the fern as it runs.

Stone over stone, Cuthman has spoken out
His faith to his mother. She has been comforted
A little; begins to believe in her son.
He has made her clumsy rhymes to laugh at.
She has tried to tell him stories of his grandmother,
But it is hard to talk buffeted by a cart.

After these miles, at last when the day leans
On the wall, at last when the vagrant hour flops
In the shade, they found a protected place, a ground
Where limbs and prayers could stretch between root and
Root, between root and sky; and they slept under curfew
Or Cuthman slept. His mother was chasing fears
Until daylight. 'What is rustling in the grass?
What shakes in the tree? What is hiding in
The shadow?' And Cuthman said, 'God is there.
God is waiting with us.'

Stone over stone, in the thin morning, they plod
Again, until they come to a field where mowers
Sweep their scythes under the dry sun.

CUTHMAN: I was alone by the unattended pillar,
Mourning the bereaved air that lay so quiet
Between walls; hungry for hammer-blows.
And the momentous hive that once was there.
And when I prayed my voice slid to the ground
Like a crushed pediment.
There was a demolition written over
The walls, and dogs rummaged in the foundations,
And picnic parties laughed on a heap of stone.
But gradually I was aware of some one in
The doorway and turned my eyes that way and saw
Carved out of the sunlight a man who stood
Watching me, so still that there was not
Other such stillness anywhere on the earth,
So still that the air seemed to leap
At his side. He came towards me, and the sun
Flooded its banks and flowed across the shadow.
He asked me why I stood alone. His voice
Hovered on memory with open wings
And drew itself up from a chine of silence
As though it had longtime lain in a vein of gold.
I told him: It is the king-post.
He stretched his hand upon it. At his touch
It lifted to its place. There was no sound.
I cried out, and I cried at last 'Who are you?'
I heard him say 'I was a carpenter' . . .
    (*They fall upon their knees.*)
There under the bare walls of our labour
Death and life were knotted in one strength
Indivisible as root and sky.

THE PEOPLE OF SOUTH ENGLAND:
The candle of our story has burnt down
And Cuthman's life is puffed like a dandelion
Into uncertain places. But the hand
Still leads the earth to drink at the sky, and still
The messenger rides into the city of leaves
Under the gradual fires of September;
The Spring shall hear, the Winter shall be wise

To warning of aconite and freezing lily,
And all shall watch the augur of a star
And learn their stillness from a stiller heaven.
And what of us who upon Cuthman's world
Have grafted progress without lock or ratchet?
What of us who have to catch up, always
To catch up with the high-powered car, or with
The unbalanced budget, to cope with competition,
To weather the sudden thunder of the uneasy
Frontier? We also loom with the earth
Over the waterways of space. Between
Our birth and death we may touch understanding
As a moth brushes a window with its wing.

Who shall question then
Why we lean our bicycle against a hedge
And go into the house of God?
Who shall question
That coming out from our doorways
We have discerned a little, we have known
More than the gossip that comes to us over our gates.

from Venus Observed

DUKE. Shall I be sorry for myself? In mortality's name
    I'll be sorry for myself. Branches and boughs,
    Brown hills, the valleys faint with brume,
    A burnish on the lake; mile by mile
    It's all a unison of ageing,
    The landscape's all in tune, in a falling cadence,
    All decaying. And nowhere does it have to hear
    The quips of spring, or, when so nearing its end,
    Have to bear the merry mirth of May.
    How fortunate to grow in the crow-footed woods,
    Eh, Reedbeck? But I see you're anxious to sleep.

REEDBECK. I? No, no; I'll never go to sleep
   Again to-night, much too disturbed.
   Don't know what to suggest I make of anything.
   I only hope a quiet dignity
   Will meet the case. Civilization is simply
   (If I had to define it) simply dignity,
   Simply simple dignity; but then
   Sons and daughters come into it, most lovable,
   Most difficult, and unexpected combustion,
   And so forth and so forth. Now le Roi Soleil,
   How many children did he have? One legitimate,
   Several illegitimate . . . le Duc de Maine,
   La Duchesse de Chartres . . .

DUKE. Shall I be happy for myself?
   In the name of existence I'll be happy for myself.
   Why, Reedbeck, how marvellous it is to moulder.
   Think how you would have felt when you were lying
   Grubbing in your mother's womb,
   With only a wall to look at,
   If you could have seen in your embryonic eye
   The realm of bryony, sloes, rose-hips,
   And a hedge's ruin, a golden desuetude,
   A countryside like a drowned angel
   Lying in shallow water, every thorn
   Tendering a tear. Think, Reedbeck,
   Think of the wonder of such glimmering woe;
   How in a field of milk-white haze the lost
   Apollo glows and wanders towards noon;
   The wind-blown webs are brighter,
   The rolling apples warmer than the sun.
   Heavens! you would have cried, the womb
   Echoing round you: These are the heavens, and I,
   Reedbeck, am stillborn. Would you not?

REEDBECK [*waking slightly*]. And la Duchesse de Condé, I
   think.

DUKE. So with ourselves; imagine: to have the sensation
Of nearness of sight, shortness of breath,
Palpitation, creaking in the joints,
Shootings, stabbings, lynching of the limbs,
A sudden illumination of lumbago.
What a rich world of sensation to achieve,
What infinite variety of being.
Is it not?

John Galsworthy
(1867–1933)

Galsworthy lived in a beautiful greystone Elizabethan style house in the picturesque village of Bury, near Amberley, which he bought as soon as he first saw it for £9,000 in 1926. He lived there for seven years, completing *The Forsyte Saga*, and wrote affectionately of the countryside around. He participated in many local acts of charity, always unobtrusive, towards local residents, and although he died in his London house, his son scattered his ashes on the Downs at Bury Hill, where he was wont to take his morning ride. The deeply felt wish of his verses was happily obeyed.

Herman Ould

A Memoir of John Galsworthy

I remember walking with Galsworthy, a year or two before his death, over the Sussex Downs. It was a grey, windy afternoon: the previous day it had rained unceasingly and we had little hope of returning dry. The inevitable dog accompanied us, but was left to pursue its own interests, which were many. We walked briskly; J.G., although in the middle sixties, was as vigorous as a young man. Pausing on a ridge above Bury, we looked over the sweep of the Downs, silvery and remote, reserved and unspectacular, placid and curiously self-possessed. Not unlike Galsworthy himself, I thought.

'You wouldn't see that anywhere except in England,' he said; and we tried to discover what it is about the Downs which so distinguishes them from all other hills and stamps them as peculiarly English.

'There's something clean, swept . . .' and he added, almost apologetically, 'spiritual about them.' This is what he wrote:

'On the spur of the Sussex Downs, inland from Nettlefold, stands a beech-grove. The traveller who enters it out of the heat and brightness, takes off the shoes of his spirit before its sanctity; and reaching the centre, across the clean beech-mat, he sits refreshing his brow with air, and silence. For the flowers of sunlight on the ground under those branches are pale and rare, no insects hum, the birds are almost mute. And close to the border-trees are the quiet milk-white sheep, in congregation, escaping from the noon heat. Here, above the fields and dwellings, above the ceaseless network of men's doings, and the vapour of their talk, the traveller feels solemnity. All seems conveying dignity – the great white clouds moving their wings above him, the faint longing murmur of the boughs, and in far distance, the sea. And for a space his restlessness and fear know the peace of God.'

John Galsworthy

Scatter My Ashes

Scatter my ashes!
  Let them be free to the air,
  Soaked in the sunlight and rain,
  Scatter, with never a care
  Whether you find them again.
  Let them be grey in the dawn,
  Bright if the noontime be bright,
  And when night's curtain is drawn
  Starry and dark with the night.
  Let the birds find them and take
  Lime for their nests, and the beast,
  Nibbling the grizzled grass, make
  Merry with salt to his feast.
Scatter my ashes!
  Hereby I make it a trust;
  I in no grave be confined,
  Mingle my dust with the dust,
  Give me in fee to the wind!
    Scatter my ashes!

Patrick Garland
(1935–   )

Both of these poems, published in *Encounter*, 1986/1987, are heavily influenced by the seascape of The Manhood Peninsula, the triangle of land which extends beyond Chichester harbour, enclosed by East and West Wittering. The ancient site of the first South Saxon settlements lies beneath scattered hamlets, bird-sanctuaries and desolate estuaries – names with Saxon roots buried within them, Bracklesham (Braccia's hëam), Brimfast (Breon's fëost), Cakeham (Caccia's hëam), form a necklace of small seaside villages. It is rumoured that the original Selsey Cathedral lies far out to sea, under the mile-long tides. Legend claims that the bells of St Wilfrid's original spire can be heard on winter nights, when there is a high swell. Not true of course, but several acres of the beach washed by the high tide are known as The Bishop's Deer Park, and some years ago fossilised antlers were occasionally dug out of the sand.

Bill Wyman was the Stones ace-scorer. His diary code for a night with a girl was 'stuck in fog'.

Stuck in Fog

This woman writes to say I use dis-interested
When I mean *un* – a sluttish trick of speech;
Dragging my feet in muddy plough detested
Across late August fields I end up on a beach:
The tides are out by now, and acres lie behind
Of rape and pillage; where the curlews screech
Stink-horn and fox-skunk bristle in the wind –
My heart is drab and guilty, out of reach.

It sticks to me, like sea-fret, autumn fly,
And fog-horns off The Deer Park sound like 'boring'.
Ships don't strand there now – the sea's too high.
So sweeten my imagination, fetch the borage
Good apothecary, for this amatory scoring –
When love is stuck in fog, lust has to forage.

The Witterings

Oh, there is withering all right: of that no doubt.
The bishop's deer-park under sea, and sucking out
The debris left behind excursion trips –
A trash of cockles, plastic water-wings, and bottled stout.

Seffrid's skeletal deer hoof-print the mud
At ebb, the Brimfast massacres, brick fields daubed in blood!
Where Poplars Seven with rape and mustard blow
Braccia's raiders fathomed under flood.

Beneath these footings lurk rich mysteries:
Ring-hoard has been found there, and the elder trees
Have felt the Saxon settler rasp his axe,
Shaded the Regni, sprawling at their ease.

Now autumn stubble burns: a spitting cage
Of thorns and hedgerows, black and sweet, engage,
With heaped-up skies bent westward, all downwind,
Dense with their anger, red in rage, in rage.

Robert Gittings
(1911–1992)

Robert Gittings, who died in 1992, was born in Portsmouth, the son of a surgeon. He came to live in East Dean, Chichester, anticipating the arrival of his great friends, Christopher and Phyl Fry, who arrived in the same village in July 1967. For twenty years and more he worked as a BBC producer, often creating dramatic or literary scripts, which he directed himself. He is best remembered for his masterly works of scholarship on John Keats, and Thomas Hardy, for which he received, deservedly, international recognition and academic awards. It was his personal research and learned observation which first drew attention to the close connection between the monuments in Chichester Cathedral, also the tiny eccentric chapel at Stansted, (devoted to the conversion of the Jews by Lewis Way in the early nineteenth century) and the visit of Keats to Chichester in 1819. The introduction to 'The Ode on the Eve of St Agnes' confirms this. Gittings' poems, drawn from the richness of several published collections, commemorate two figures who spent their last years in Sussex: W. H. Hudson, who lies in Broadwater Cemetery, Worthing, and Edward Elgar, whose enchanting cottage at Fittleworth is occupied today by a locally distinguished composer. Derelict for years, I remember visiting it in the 1980s, and was keenly reminded of the melancholy of much of the last quintet Elgar composed there. It's far happier now.

Elgar

When Land of Hope and Glory blared advance
To muddy Tartarus, and all those men –
Boys really – smothered to that booming strain
The brass pomped out in barrack circumstance,

You hid, beneath Edwardian elegance,
The small-boy heart dreading small-town disdain,
The shopman's son, ashamed to feel a stain
Worse than the wounds they suffered there in France.

You bluffed it through, honours and titles, all
An English gentleman should seem, complete,
Yet those sad chords at each packed festival
Betrayed you, the composer of a grief
So deep, not even a million marching feet
Could drown that last enigma of your life.

Roman Villa in England

All the pale woodland seems
Strange where the sunbeams cross;
Mauve autumn crocus teems
On pavement caked with moss;
Lost in a valley of streams,
Whose voices choke its loss,
The Roman villa gleams
Beside the broken fosse.

Pillar and column lie
Leaf-logged and sodden here,
Denied their daylight by
This northland atmosphere,
Lacking the torrid, high,
Sharp, blue, expressly clear,
Supreme Italian sky
Their owner found so dear,

But could not see; this was
His miniature of Rome,
The bubble in his glass,
The spectrum of a home.

Hopeful, he brought to pass
Buildings now brown with loam,
Mosaic flecked with grass,
Speckled with weedy foam.

The altar that a god
Once guarded now is gone;
Where the white image stood
Coarse lichens eat the stone;
The temple in the wood
Is worshipped now by none
But beetle, worm, and brood
Of weird inhuman bone.

And if the gods could not,
No more could men remain;
Early the doors were shut,
And early came the rain,
The damp, the mould, the rot,
The sunken beam, the strain
On delicate plaster, blot
On blot and stain on stain,

Till winter's shaking head,
Or summer's twitching frown,
Precarious tremor sped
And stripped the whole house down,
Its owner long since dead,
And Rome, without a crown,
Impotent, blindfold, led
To ruins of its own.

Not even empire, then,
Colony, trade, or war
Will cut secure for men
Footholds of what they are;
The wreck of what has been
Only remains, to scar
The unreflecting green
With flakes of glistening spar.

The Grave of W. H. Hudson
Broadwater Cemetery, Worthing

The plain stone says that his body is buried here
    In this population of crosses,
But indeed the marble already was over his head,
    And the forests of brick had trapped him
  Long before he was dead.

The lanes whose hedges are iron railings, whose paths
    Are lines and blocks of pavement,
Had wounded the feet and draggled the featherknit life;
    A forty years' wilderness suffered,
  Now he lies by his wife

Cramped and crowded even in death. The grave
    Is narrow; but men when dying
Do not imagine what moralists afterwards say.
    He was old, outworn, and tired,
  Past the end of his day,

Yet to live, not to die, was still his love. He saw
    Spring, summer, autumn, winter,
Holding out hands to him, every season, with wing,
    Petal, fur, and insect glitter,
  Bright with the living thing,

The multiform gender of being. What then to him
    Was the infinite Nothing,
Whose promise he did not believe, but of whose acts
    He was daily warden and worshipper,
  Miracles known as facts? –

The passage of midnight pinions across the moon,
    The air with a rustling and creaking

Filled to an overbrimming pitch unheard,
        Instinct beyond all nature,
Beyond all reason, the sense of a migrant bird –

The least low many-headed chalk-fed flower
        That stains the short-cropped downland,
How it writhes and fingers for roothold, how it breaks
        Through gravel and flinty boulder
Beyond all strength in itself for the soil it seeks, –

The rush of the world through dark blue space, observed
        By the night-still dew-cold watcher
On top of some turning hill, as the waited dawn
        Rolls into gold and purple,
While under the west the stars are silently drawn. –

What, beside these, is the bare unpromising grave,
        The briar-rose corners planted
To graft an air of wildness on formal pride,
        The tomb of nature's lover? –
While still the great passion sweeps and thunders outside,

High in the air and deep in the sea – as on
        The long green restless pampas
Where he was reared, a searing breath would send
        A world of thistledown flying,
Seed-dust of his beginning: and such be his end.

Charles Goring

The monarch of the South Down range, crowned by its circle of beeches, is Chanctonbury Ring. It appears to have an air of the pagan 'ancient' about it, but was merely a circle of respectable saplings when planted in 1760 by Charles Goring of Wiston House (pronounced Wisson). When he was a very old man himself in 1828, he was able to write these lines of great contentment, looking up from the valley below.

Chanctonbury Ring

How oft around thy Ring, sweet Hill,
  A Boy, I used to play,
And form my plans to plant thy top
  On some auspicious day.
How oft among thy broken turf
  With what delight I trod,
With what delight I placed those twigs
  Beneath thy maiden sod.
And then an almost hopeless wish
  Would creep within my breast,
Oh! could I live to see thy top
  In all its beauty dressed.
That time's arrived; I've had my wish,
  And lived to eighty-five;
I'll thank my God who gave such grace
  As long as e'er I live.
Still when the morning Sun in Spring,
  Whilst I enjoy my sight,
Shall gild thy new-clothed Beech and sides,
  I'll view thee with delight.

William Hayley
(1745–1820)

Hayley 1779

Epitaph on a Felpham Blacksmith

My sledge and hammer lie reclined;
My bellows too have lost their wind;
My fire's extinct; my forge decay'd,
And in the dust my vice is laid;
My coal is spent, my iron gone;
The nails are driven – my work is done.

William Ernest Henley
(1849–1903)

William Henley

Auguste Rodin's leonine head of William Ernest Henley is in the National Portrait Gallery, but few people take much notice of it now. He was one of that now-archaic group of celebrities, once a commonplace in literary circles, named the Men of Letters. The combination of striking nobility of countenance, and giant body, together with a crippled frame, inspired his friend Robert Louis Stevenson to model his pirate of genius, Long John Silver, on Henley. He resembled the buccaneer in character also, vigorous and unreasonable in his opinions, quarrelsome and benevolent, eloquent and impassioned. He shared with Kipling (whom he first published in his weekly magazine) a profound dislike of the Wilde set, and the Decadents around the Café Royal. His favoured haunt in the Eighties and early Nineties was Solferino's in Regent Street, a gathering-place of robust and tough-minded journalists and artists (Whistler and Sickert among them), whom Max Beerbohm somewhat dismissingly described as 'the Henley Regatta'. 'It was the sight of your maimed strength and masterfulness that begot Silver in *Treasure Island*,' wrote Stevenson, a portrait Henley never altogether approved of, and his relations with Stevenson (whom he met in a tubercular clinic in Edinburgh) were scarcely serene, and finally, they were estranged. Restless in disposition, he lived mainly around London, only coming to rest in Worthing towards the end of his short life. He sought out the Sussex coast for its light and clean air and found the correct form of repose he was seeking in a typical Victorian villa in a secluded part of Worthing, at the corner of Chesswood Road. He was a lover of England, and a lover of the Sussex countryside, and much of his finest verse is included in his last book of poems, *Hawthorn and Lavender*. There is much to admire in his writing, out of date and unfashionable though it might be, especially his touching autobiographical poem 'Shoreham River'. He made one final move to Woking, where he died, in 1903, seemingly much, much older, but merely fifty-four. It is fitting that his Worthing house became first of all St George's Hotel, and is now, like much of the rest of Worthing, an old people's home. Rather unexpectedly, considering its contemporary reputation, Henley admired Worthing, not so much for its sunshine, but for 'its up-to-datedness. I knew Worthing was pulsing harmoniously with the striking hour directly I took my first walk through its streets.'

His most famous lines are as familiar to pre-war public schoolboys as those of Kipling's *Recessional*:

> It matters not how strait the Gate,
> How charged with punishments the scroll,
> I am the Master of my Fate
> I am the Captain of my Soul.

The Dedication To His Wife

> Ask me not how they came,
> These songs of love and death,
> These dreams of a futile stage,
> These thumb-nails seen in the street:
> Ask me not how nor why,
> But take them for your own,
> Dear Wife of twenty years,
> Knowing so, who so well?
> You it was made the man
> That made these songs of love,
> Death, and the trivial rest:
> So that, your love elsewhere,
> These songs, for bad or good,
> How should they ever have been?

from The Ballade of Dead Actors

> The curtain falls, the play is played:
>   The Beggar packs beside the Beau:
> The Monarch troops, and troops the Maid;

The Thunder huddles with the Snow.
   Where are the revellers high and low?
The clashing swords? The lover's call?
   The dancers gleaming row on row?
Into the night go one and all.

To H. B. M. W.

Where forlorn sunsets flare and fade
   On desolate sea and lonely sand,
Out of the silence and the shade
   What is the voice of strange command
Calling you still, as friend calls friend
   With love that cannot brook delay,
To rise and follow the ways that wend
   Over the hills and far away.

Hark in the city, street on street,
   A roaring reach of death and life,
Of vortices that clash and fleet
   And ruin in appointed strife,
Hark to it calling, calling clear,
   Calling until you cannot stay
From dearer things than your own most dear
   Over the hills and far away.

Out of the sound of the ebb-and-flow,
   Out of the sight of lamp and star,
It calls you where the good winds blow,
   And the unchanging meadows are:
From faded hopes and hopes agleam,
   It calls you, calls you night and day
Beyond the dark into the dream
   Over the hills and far away.

The Old Boat

In Shoreham River, hurrying down
To the live sea,
By working, marrying, breeding, Shoreham Town,
Breaking the sunset's wistful and solemn dream,
An old, black rotter of a boat
Past service to the labouring, tumbling flote,
Lay stranded in mid-stream;
With a horrid list, a frightening lapse from the line,
That made me think of legs and a broken spine;
Soon, all too soon,
Ungainly and forlorn to lie
Full in the eye
Of the cynical, discomfortable moon
That, as I looked, stared from the fading sky,
A clown's face flour'd for work. And by and by
The wide-winged sunset waned and waned;
The lean night-wind crept westward, chilling and sighing;
The poor old hulk remained,
Stuck helpless in mid-ebb. And I knew why –
Why, as I looked, my heart felt crying.
For, as I looked, the good green earth seemed dying –
Dying or dead;
And, as I looked on the old boat, I said:
'Dear God, it's I!'

The Howling Boys

The Howling Boys of Sussex turned out each year to ensure that
fruit trees would escape the attention of the evil spirits and
provide a satisfactory crop in the coming season. Dressed in an
assortment of strange clothes, they would arrive after dark and
request permission of the owners of the trees to perform with
their cows' horns, drums, and other noise-making implements.
Gathering around each tree they would begin with an ancient
ditty, something along these lines:

Stand fast root, bear well top,
Pray the Gods send us a good howling crop.
Every twig, apples big,
Every bough, apples enow,
Hats full, caps full, my pockets full too.

Tony Wales

W. H. Hudson
(1841–1922)

W. H. Hudson, the naturalist, wrote no poetry, sadly, but extolled the life on the Downs in 1899, when he moved to Goring-on-Sea and began writing *Nature in Downland*. All his life he passionately admired Richard Jefferies, and began writing in the very house in which Jefferies had died – it was his fervent wish to be buried in the same graveyard, Broadwater Cemetery, close to 'the prose poet of England's fields and woodlands'. It is fitting they should be close together now, in these few following pages. Interestingly, Jefferies writes about the same experience of crumbling a handful of earth through his fingers, as Kipling and Edward Thomas – and asks, like Galsworthy, for his ashes to be scattered, but in his case, a request not granted.

The Living Garment of the Downs

Here one may see the corn reaped with sickles in the ancient way; and, better still, the wheat carried from the field in wains drawn by two or three couples of great, long-horned, black oxen. One wonders which of the three following common sights of the Sussex Downs carries us further back in time; the cluster of cottages, with church and farm buildings that form the village nestling in the valley, and seen from above appearing as a mere red spot in the prospect; the grey-clad shepherd, crook in hand, standing motionless on some vast green slope, his grey, rough-haired sheep-dog resting at his feet; or the team of coal-black, long-horned oxen drawing the plough or carrying the corn.

The little rustic village in the deep dene, with its two or three hundred inhabitants, will probably outlast London, or at all events London's greatness; and the stolid shepherd with his dog at his feet will doubtless stand watching his flock on the hillside for some thousands of years to come; but these great, slow, patient oxen cannot go on dragging the plough much longer; the wonder is that they have continued to the present time. One gazes lovingly at them, and on leaving them casts many a longing, lingering look behind, fearing that after a little while their place will know them no more.

Richard Jefferies
(1848–1887)

The Sussex Downs

And as Mr Dudeney, the South Down shepherd said, 'the closer you lie to the turf the more you're apt to see things'. Besides the mind sometimes is better for being spread and bleached. It wants the simplest experience and simplest delights. Hear Richard Jefferies:

> There, alone, I went down to the sea. I stood where the foam came to my feet, and looked out over the sunlit waters. The great earth bearing the richness of the harvest, and its hills golden with corn, was at my back; its strength and firmness under me. The great sun shone above, the wide sea was before me, the wind came sweet and strong from the waves . . . I rubbed out some of the wheat in my hands, I took up a piece of clod and crumbled it in my fingers – it was a joy to touch it – I held my hand so that I could see the sunlight gleam on the slightly soft surface of the skin. The earth and sun were like my flesh and blood, and the air of the sea life.

The literary pilgrim will not fail to seek the grave of Jefferies at Broadwater. He died at Goring, hard by, in 1887. 'If I had my own way after death,' wrote Jefferies in *The Story of my Heart*, 'I would be burned on a pyre of pinewood, open to the air, and placed on the summit of the hills. Then let my ashes be scattered abroad – not collected in an urn – freely sown wide and broadcast.'

Both Jefferies and Hudson are apt to romanticise the landscape (but not the life of Sussex shepherds) which was civilized enough. In order that the image of early-twentieth-century

Sussex is neither too pastoral, nor too serene, Horace Walpole and Chancellor Cowper paint a more realistic picture of life on the road, before the invention of Southern Rail:

Horace Walpole

To George Montagu (1749)

Mr Chute and I returned from our expedition miraculously well, considering all our distresses. If you love good roads, conveniences, good inns, plenty of postilions and horses, be so kind as never to go into Sussex. We thought ourselves in the northest part of England; the whole county has a Saxon air, and the inhabitants are savage, as if King George the Second was the first monarch of the East Angles. Coaches grow there no more than balm and spices: we were forced to drop our post-chaise, that resembled nothing so much as harlequin's calash, which was occasionally a chaise or a baker's cart. We journeyed over alpine mountains drenched in clouds, and thought of harlequin again, when he was driving the chariot of the sun through the morning clouds, and was so glad to hear the *aqua vitae* man crying a dram . . . I have set up my staff, and finished my pilgrimages for this year. Sussex is a great damper of curiosity.

Lord Chancellor Cowper

To His Wife (1690)

I write to you from this place as soon as I arrive, to tell you I have come off without hurt, both in my going and return through the Sussex ways, which are bad and ruinous beyond imagination. I vow 'tis a melancholy consideration that mankind will inhabit such a heap of dirt for a poor livelihood. The country is a sink about fourteen miles broad, which receives all the water that falls from two long ranges on both sides of it; and not being furnished with convenient draining, is kept moist and soft by the water till the middle of a dry summer, which is only able to make it tolerable to ride for a short time. The same day I entered Surrey, a fine champagne country, dry and dusty as if the season of the year had shifted in a few hours from winter to midsummer.

1690

Nicki Jackowska

In her recent collection of poems, *News from the Brighton Front*, her fifth, Nicki Jackowska, who has lived in Brighton for some years, takes from its title a literal location of her home-town, raffish, life-affirming, political and confrontational. Her powerful and original poems have some of the kaleidoscopic vitality everybody associates with the sea-front capital of mid-Sussex. 'News from the Brighton Front' and 'Farewell to Brighton' are the first and concluding parts of a long poem capturing the vibrant moods which lie beneath the sleazy town of Regency façades, dilapidated piers, antique-markets, slot-machines, and prize-every-time amusement arcades; a community in its own right, ignoring the external life of day-trippers and foreign students, proceeding in its own idiosyncratic style.

News from the Brighton Front

The man takes a stone.
He grunts. A chip flies from its flank.
He mixes metaphors.
It winks blue and purple under the crazy pier.

The woman takes a stone.
Its blue skin is startled by her scarlet nail.
She traces a name in its cool fist.
The letter grumbles on her bag's seabed.

Between her feet, sea gnashes, her silver heel
knocks on wood. Waterskin catches her face,
throws it back. Only fish have tunnel vision.
She strolls the pier tossing her hooks overboard.

Honeyman eating candyfloss in a blue striped
blazer. Honeyman in a check suit that yells
summer. Honeyman with nothing in his pockets,
tilted like a liner, waving to the fat thighs
with a pale unburned hand.

You are all used up, she tells the fruit-machine.
Orange peel shredded from the sun's fracture.
Man under the pier tied up with string. Sun
sticking his limbs together. Soon his face will
shine out of its bag, thirsty for fruit.

The woman sees that he is thirsty.
She asks him the time. A watchface spins
in his eye's cyclone. I never stay long
enough, he says.
An hour crawls between her legs. She leaves
him straddled on the weedy groyne.

Going hunting. The crazy pierstakes.
Hunting a crack in the day. Through which
he may pour fish-oil and sweat and the voice
of a romping sea.
Going hunting. Trying to escape from his
string vest. Looking for tunnels into the
light. Her skirts up round the motorway.
It winks blue as a stone.

The man is selling monkeys. Their felt jackets
shout at the strollers like parakeets. Pavements
hot as a jungle. The monkeys chatter, wondering
at the origin of species. Ice-cream runs from
their mouths like the tongues of lilies.
Summer spilling.

The sea wakes first, a thin silver needle.
Then the man breathes earth in through paper
shoes. On the promenade, in the white hotel,
she wakes next in her ruffled bed.
Her sheets itch.

At coffee time she sits in her deckchair
reading the penguin book of contemporary
beetroot recipes.

I've reached rock-bottom she tells her friend,
he's gone back to his wife. The gull flies
too high screaming in ecstasy. He has the
wings for it.

Another fish says her friend, another
pale face coming up out of the tank.
What kind do you want in this aquarium,
dogfish or razoreel. They swim the
promenade, noses against glass.

Who needs a Martian eye. Or uncut videos.
Behind the roasting knuckle, each sunbather
preserves an inwardness of palm. Where the
world tickles in.

The Grand Hotel is missing a couple of floors,
a gash in its proud flank.
Sightseers along the promenade, missing a
couple of floors.
Between the death and the death, a lift-shaft
of silence.
Nostalgic rubble hastily shuffles into
the gap.

Boadicea rides again. Roll up!
Her warship cleaves the tired seafront air. The
papers drum up an audience, slot another cylinder
into the penny machine. Cheap at the price.
And the land has a hole in its flank and water
in her leaky shoes.

Marks and Spencers rise to the occasion. Fly a
drip-dry flag. At seven am he pats the pocket
of his silk pyjamas. No credit card. Still the

shirts fly from cellophane to comfort him and
blouses drift across well-heeled breasts to
comfort him.
We do not hesitate to clothe our leaders, says
the manager, unlocking his plate-glass doors
two hours early.

Money down the drain, down the penny-machine,
pouring from the till.
Someone reverses the video and Marks and
Spencers
clothes the cabinet. Consolation for a hole in
the side.
We are glad the emperor has a new suit of clothes
says the manager, stroking his assets and his
salesgirl with a shot-silk paw.

She has a hole in her bag where the letter falls
through and her boss pays for the orchestra to play
her evening wide, and the hole in the white hotel
says the critic is where the sightseers crowd on in,
too many of them, the ship splits a seam and begins
its slow march to the sea-bed.

Do not go naked into the conference chamber,
clothe the cabinet of curiosities, speciality
of Brighton, the museum preserves a discrete
shade.

Moving towards winter. Beginning to gather, tanks
on the pierhead in spite of clement weather.
Woman in indian summer deckchair reading of
      penguins.
Behind her the Grand Hotel with a hole in its face.
Behind her Boadicea with a hole in her heart. Behind
her the president, a hole in his celluloid.

I don't like this movie, he says, there's a frame
missing where the people ought to be.
Someone left the Indians on the cutting-room
floor.

Behind her the Grand Hotel where leaders danced
waving their gilt-edged securities. Someone said
they're the guardians of the British way of life.
Which is also to say brutal wish to lacerate, or
bomb with love, or even best writers of lies.
She prefers boastful witnesses of limpets, having
one stuck in her shoe. And writes it.

Graffiti under the pier. They're surprised when
the shadows speak, these leaders, it interrupts
the pantomime. Thought Indians were extinct,
won't
they ever learn, we're in charge of the cutting-room
floor.

Stone-scratchers that rise up against the town's
cataract and cut its blind face.
It takes an operation to remove a root.

In charge of summer, winter, and in charge of
words for it. The postcard flies in the teeth
of the ice-cap on the other side.
Though her skin's still seasonal.
It hits the president on the chin. He swats
a fly.

In Gatsby-under-Wold he leans to adjust the silver
nipple of his radio set. In Brighton she stretches
to turn down the volume of fish-sound that keeps
escaping from aquariums.
Between them, a continent rises. They give each
other credit for not creating it.
Decide not to consult over the means of exploration.

In the early hours of friday october twelve nineteen
eighty-four, gulls scatter. She wakes in her bed
at two forty-five and asks him if he's locked the
car. The timer creeps to zero, the end of dialogue.

The prime minister leaves the bathroom and launders
her speech. You can smell salt in the backstreets.
He and she fuck across the distances.
They say the fuse was set a century ago.

Farewell to Brighton

All that shingle ringing against its mate
and the sea overlapping into her thighs' fork.
She cases the pier, left behind when dawn creaks in
and celebration dries like an old prune
nobody's choice of breakfast.

And all the landladies close their doors
in a ricochet along the front
saying no, no, in a great chorus of squawks.
The parrots bite her fingers saying 'pretty'.

It is a long time, the pier was always thus
never without its damp undertow
a great fall-down from that bright stair
to paradise, a ruff of pink at the waist
a high white shoe; all tumbled, scuffed
and wanton in the bleary drift of moon
when dawn washes it, the sky scouring
her seafront sutra, her pink net petticoat
awash through all its wires; a long time.

All that shingle; still the stones mutter
against tides, against her heavy dream-swell.

Slowly they leave, the song's belovèd
the one who sang it out; going north or west
leaving the crazy pier, the change machine
the frantic rattle of a seaside town counting its cost.

Brighton has always been a haven for great music-hall artists in retirement. Max Miller, in the last months of his life, could be found seated in one of the shelters on Brighton Pier staring at the Channel. He said to a friend who used to keep him company: 'Look at the sea, son, look at the sea. Full of hate, son, full of hate.'

In vulgar tongue, a hundred years ago, a Brighton man used to be called 'a Brighton Jug'.

John Keats
(1795–1821)

Keats 1819

According to his biographer, Robert Gittings (who lived in East Dean), Keats arrived in Chichester in January 1819, having just met Fanny Brawne in Hampstead, and even more recently, having been involved in a romance of some strength and intoxication, with a mysterious and elusive woman known as Mrs Isabella Jones. It is principally Gittings' suggestion that the combination of these two heady experiences, fresh in his head, and affected by the medieval atmosphere of Chichester Cathedral, lay at the root of his inspiration for the remarkable narrative poem, 'The Eve of St Agnes', which Keats composed at that time. His throwaway reference to 'the little poem he wrote on thin paper' dates the composition very securely. The ode not only captures the wintry mood of the archaic city, but introduces an almost cinematic vision of a strange sensuous narrative, captured on the threshold of life and death, of dream and wakefulness. Its imagery, shot throughout with Shakespearean resonances, has about it a kind of frozen languor, an unusual and eerie mixture, which makes Keats' poem one of the most original in our language, and explains why it is quoted in full.

The red-brick house Keats stayed in belonged to the Dilke family. Mr Dilke was a retired Navy Office civil servant, at a time when Chichester was a prosperous mercantile city, where grain-ships sailed into the security of Chichester Harbour. On a personal note, I can never forget the shock I had some twenty years ago, when I was rehearsing a play for the theatre in Chichester, in a former public house in Eastgate Square. Casually looking out of the window, during a *longueur* in the rehearsal, my eye lazily fell on the barber's shop on the first floor of a handsome red-bricked Georgian house, on the far side of the street. My eye travelled up and above to a room where a man sat in a chair, with towels tucked about him, and I saw – with what Philip Larkin calls 'a sharp, tender shock' – a plaque on the wall which reads: 'Here John Keats began to write The Eve of St Agnes, 1819'.

Keats returned to London in the middle of February, and revisited Isabella Jones with the concluded version of the poem, and presented it to his publisher, John Taylor, in April.

Christopher Fry tells me he always has his hair cut by that

barber, in order to sit in the very room in which Keats used to
sleep.

*From John Keats to George and Georgiana Keats, Sunday 14
Feb. – Monday 3 May, 1819.*

I say since my return from Chichester – I believe I told you I was
going thither – I was nearly a fortnight at Mr John Snook's and
a few days at old Mr Dilke's – Nothing worth speaking of
happened at either place – I took down some of the thin paper
and wrote on it a little poem call'd 'St Agnes Eve' which you
shall have as it is when I have finished the blank part of the rest
for you. I went out twice at Chichester to old Dowager card
parties. I see very little now, and very few Persons – being
almost tired of Men and things . . .

An Ode to The Eve of St Agnes

I

St Agnes' Eve – Ah, bitter chill it was!
The owl, for all his feathers, was a-cold;
The hare limp'd trembling through the frozen grass,
And silent was the flock in woolly fold:
Numb were the Beadsman's fingers, while he told
His rosary, and while his frosted breath,
Like pious incense from a censer old,
Seem'd taking flight for heaven, without a death,
Past the sweet Virgin's picture, while his prayer he saith.

II

His prayer he saith, this patient, holy man;
Then takes his lamp, and riseth from his knees,
And back returneth, meagre, barefoot, wan,

Along the chapel aisle by slow degrees:
The sculptured dead, on each side, seem to freeze,
Emprison'd in black, purgatorial rails:
Knights, ladies, praying in dumb orat'ries,
He passeth by; and his weak spirit fails
To think how they may ache in icy hoods and mails.

III

Northward he turneth through a little door,
And scarce three steps, ere Music's golden tongue
Flatter'd to tears this aged man and poor;
But no – already had his deathbell rung:
The joys of all his life were said and sung:
His was harsh penance on St Agnes' Eve:
Another way he went, and soon among
Rough ashes sat he for his soul's reprieve,
And all night kept awake, for sinners' sake to grieve.

IV

That ancient Beadsman heard the prelude soft;
And so it chanced, for many a door was wide,
From hurry to and fro. Soon, up aloft,
The silver, snarling trumpets 'gan to chide:
The level chambers, ready with their pride,
Were glowing to receive a thousand guests:
The carved angels, ever eager-eyed,
Star'd, where upon their heads the cornice rests,
With hair blown back, and wings put cross-wise on their
    breasts.

V

At length burst in the argent revelry,
With plume, tiara, and all rich array,
Numerous as shadows haunting fairily
The brain, new stuff'd, in youth, with triumphs gay
Of old romance. These let us wish away,
And turn, sole-thoughted, to one Lady there,
Whose heart had brooded, all that wintry day,
On love, and wing'd St Agnes' saintly care,
As she had heard old dames full many times declare.

VI

They told her how, upon St Agnes' Eve,
Young virgins might have visions of delight,
And soft adorings from their loves receive
Upon the honey'd middle of the night,
If ceremonies due they did aright;
As, supperless to bed they must retire,
And couch supine their beauties, lily white;
Nor look behind, nor sideways, but require
Of Heaven with upward eyes for all that they desire.

VII

Full of this whim was thoughtful Madeline:
The music, yearning like a God in pain,
She scarcely heard: her maiden eyes divine,
Fix'd on the floor, saw many a sweeping train
Pass by – she heeded not at all: in vain
Came many a tiptoe, amorous cavalier,
And back retired; not cool'd by high disdain,
But she saw not: her heart was otherwhere:
She sigh'd for Agnes' dreams, the sweetest of the year.

VIII

She danced along with vague, regardless eyes,
Anxious her lips, her breathing quick and short:
The hallow'd hour was near at hand: she sighs
Amid the timbrels, and the throng'd resort
Of whisperers in anger, or in sport;
'Mid looks of love, defiance, hate, and scorn,
Hoodwink'd with faery fancy; all amort,
Save to St Agnes and her lambs unshorn,
And all the bliss to be before to-morrow morn.

IX

So, purposing each moment to retire,
She linger'd still. Meantime, across the moors,
Had come young Porphyro, with heart on fire
For Madeline. Beside the portal doors,
Buttress'd from moonlight, stands he, and implores
All saints to give him sight of Madeline,

But for one moment in the tedious hours,
That he might gaze and worship all unseen;
Perchance speak, kneel, touch, kiss – in sooth such things have
  been.

X

He ventures in: let no buzz'd whisper tell:
All eyes be muffled, or a hundred swords
Will storm his heart, Love's fev'rous citadel:
For him, those chambers held barbarian hordes,
Hyena foemen, and hot-blooded lords,
Whose very dogs would execrations howl
Against his lineage: not one breast affords
Him any mercy, in that mansion foul,
Save one old beldame, weak in body and in soul.

XI

Ah, happy chance! the aged creature came,
Shuffling along with ivory-headed wand,
To where he stood, hid from the torch's flame,
Behind a broad hall-pillar, far beyond
The sound of merriment and chorus bland:
He startled her; but soon she knew his face,
And grasp'd his fingers in her palsied hand,
Saying, 'Mercy, Porphyro! hie thee from this place;
They are all here to-night, the whole blood-thirsty race!'

XII

'Get hence! get hence! there's dwarfish Hildebrand;
He had a fever late, and in the fit
He cursed thee and thine, both house and land:
Then there's that old Lord Maurice, not a whit
More tame for his gray hairs – Alas me! flit!
Flit like a ghost away.' – 'Ah, Gossip dear,
We're safe enough; here in this arm-chair sit,
And tell me how' – 'Good Saints! not here, not here;
Follow me, child, or else these stones will be thy bier.'

XIII

He follow'd through a lowly arched way,
Brushing the cobwebs with his lofty plume,
And as she mutter'd 'Well-a – well-a-day!'
He found him in a little moonlight room,
Pale, latticed, chill, and silent as a tomb.
'Now tell me where is Madeline,' said he,
'O tell me, Angela, by the holy loom
Which none but secret sisterhood may see,
When they St Agnes' wool are weaving piously.'

'St Agnes! Ah! it is St Agnes' Eve –
Yet men will murder upon holy days:
Thou must hold water in a witch's sieve,
And be liege-lord of all the Elves and Fays,
To venture so: it fills me with amaze
To see thee, Porphyro! – St Agnes' Eve!
God's help! my lady fair the conjuror plays
This very night: good angels her deceive!
But let me laugh awhile, I've mickle time to grieve.'

XV

Feebly she laugheth in the languid moon,
While Porphyro upon her face doth look,
Like puzzled urchin on an aged crone
Who keepeth closed a wondrous riddle-book,
As spectacled she sits in chimney nook.
But soon his eyes grew brilliant, when she told
His lady's purpose; and he scarce could brook
Tears, at the thought of those enchantments cold,
And Madeline asleep in lap of legends old.

Sudden a thought came like a full-blown rose,
Flushing his brow, and in his pained heart
Made purple riot: then doth he propose
A stratagem that makes the beldame start:
'A cruel man and impious thou art:
Sweet lady, let her pray, and sleep, and dream

Alone with her good angels, far apart
From wicked men like thee. Go, go! – I deem
Thou canst not surely be the same that thou didst seem.'

XVII

'I will not harm her, by all saints I swear,'
Quoth Porphyro: 'O may I ne'er find grace
When my weak voice shall whisper its last prayer,
If one of her soft ringlets I displace
Or look with ruffian passion in her face:
Good Angela, believe me by these tears;
Or I will, even in a moment's space,
Awake, with horrid shout, my foemen's ears,
And beard them, though they be more fang'd than wolves and
    bears.'

XVIII

'Ah! why wilt thou affright a feeble soul?
A poor, weak, palsy-stricken, churchyard thing,
Whose passing-bell may ere the midnight toll;
Whose prayers for thee, each morn and evening,
Were never miss'd.' – Thus plaining, doth she bring
A gentler speech from burning Porphyro;
So woeful, and of such deep sorrowing,
That Angela gives promise she will do
Whatever he shall wish, betide her weal or woe.

XIX

Which was, to lead him, in close secrecy,
Even to Madeline's chamber, and there hide
Him in a closet, of such privacy
That he might see her beauty unespied,
And win perhaps that night a peerless bride,
While legion'd fairies paced the coverlet,
And pale enchantment held her sleepy-eyed.
Never on such a night have lovers met,
Since Merlin paid his Demon all the monstrous debt.

XX

'It shall be as thou wishest,' said the Dame:
'All cates and dainties shall be stored there
Quickly on this feast-night: by the tambour frame
Her own lute thou wilt see: no time to spare,
For I am slow and feeble, and scarce dare
On such a catering trust my dizzy head.
Wait here, my child, with patience: kneel in prayer
The while: Ah! thou must needs the lady wed,
Or may I never leave my grave among the dead.'

XXI

So saying, she hobbled off with busy fear.
The lover's endless minutes slowly pass'd;
The dame return'd, and whispered in his ear
To follow her; with aged eyes aghast
From fright of dim espial. Safe at last,
Through many a dusky gallery, they gain
The maiden's chamber, silken, hush'd, and chaste;
Where Porphyro took covert, pleased amain.
His poor guide hurried back with agues in her brain.

XXII

Her faltering hand upon the balustrade,
Old Angela was feeling for the stair,
When Madeline, St Agnes' charmed maid,
Rose, like a mission'd spirit, unaware:
With silver taper's light, and pious care,
She turn'd, and down the aged gossip led
To a safe level matting. Now prepare,
Young Porphyro, for gazing on that bed;
She comes, she comes again, like ring-dove fray'd and fled.

XXIII

Out went the taper as she hurried in;
Its little smoke, in pallid moonshine, died:
She closed the door, she panted, all akin
To spirits of the air, and visions wide:
No utter'd syllable, or, woe betide!
But to her heart, her heart was voluble,

Paining with eloquence her balmy side;
As though a tongueless nightingale should swell
Her throat in vain, and die, heart-stifled, in her dell.

XXIV

A casement high and triple-arch'd there was,
All garlanded with carven imageries
Of fruits, and flowers, and bunches of knot-grass,
And diamonded with panes of quaint device,
Innumerable of stains and splendid dyes,
As are the tiger-moth's deep-damask'd wings;
And in the midst, 'mong thousand heraldries,
And twilight saints, and dim emblazonings,
A shielded scutcheon blush'd with blood of queens and kings.

XXV

Full on this casement shone the wintry moon
And threw warm gules on Madeline's fair breast;
As down she knelt for heaven's grace and boon;
Rose-bloom fell on her hands, together prest,
And on her silver cross soft amethyst,
And on her hair a glory, like a saint:
She seem'd a splendid angel, newly drest,
Save wings, for heaven: – Porphyro grew faint:
She knelt, so pure a thing, so free from mortal taint.

XXVI

Anon his heart revives: her vespers done,
Of all its wreathed pearls her hair she frees;
Unclasps her warmed jewels one by one;
Loosens her fragrant boddice; by degrees
Her rich attire creeps rustling to her knees
Half-hidden, like a mermaid in sea-weed,
Pensive awhile she dreams awake, and sees,
In fancy, fair St Agnes in her bed,
But dares not look behind, or all the charm is fled.

XXVII

Soon, trembling in her soft and chilly nest,
In sort of wakeful swoon, perplex'd she lay,
Until the poppied warmth of sleep oppress'd
Her soothed limbs, and soul fatigued away;

Flown, like a thought, until the morrow-day;
Blissfully haven'd both from joy and pain;
Clasp'd like a missal where swart Paynims pray;
Blinded alike from sunshine and from rain,
As though a rose should shut, and be a bud again.

XXVIII

Stolen to this paradise, and so entranced,
Porphyro gazed upon her empty dress,
And listen'd to her breathing, if it chanced
To wake into a slumberous tenderness;
Which when he heard, that minute did he bless,
And breathed himself: then from the closet crept,
Noiseless as fear in a wide wilderness,
And over the hush'd carpet, silent, stept,
And 'tween the curtains peep'd, where, lo! – how fast she slept.

XXIX

Then by the bed-side, where the faded moon
Made a dim, silver twilight, soft he set
A table, and, half anguish'd, threw thereon
A cloth of woven crimson, gold, and jet: –
O for some drowsy Morphean amulet!
The boisterous, midnight, festive clarion,
The kettle-drum, and far-heard clarionet,
Affray his ears, though but in dying tone: –
The hall door shuts again, and all the noise is gone.

XXX

And still she slept an azure-lidded sleep,
In blanched linen, smooth, and lavender'd,
While he from forth the closet brought a heap
Of candied apple, quince, and plum, and gourd
With jellies soother than the creamy curd,
And lucent syrops, tinct with cinnamon;
Manna and dates, in argosy transferr'd
From Fez; and spiced dainties, every one,
From silken Samarcand to cedar'd Lebanon.

XXXI

These delicates he heap'd with glowing hand
On golden dishes and in baskets bright
Of wreathed silver: sumptuous they stand
In the retired quiet of the night,
Filling the chilly room with perfume light. –
'And now, my love, my seraph fair, awake!
Thou art my heaven, and I thine eremite:
Open thine eyes, for meek St Agnes' sake,
Or I shall drowse beside thee, so my soul doth ache.'

Thus whispering, his warm, unnerved arm
Sank in her pillow. Shaded was her dream
By the dusk curtains: – 'twas a midnight charm
Impossible to melt as iced stream:
The lustrous salvers in the moonlight gleam;
Broad golden fringe upon the carpet lies:
It seem'd he never, never could redeem
From such a stedfast spell his lady's eyes;
So mused awhile, entoil'd in woofed phantasies.

XXXIII

Awakening up, he took her hollow lute, –
Tumultuous, – and, in chords that tenderest be,
He play'd an ancient ditty, long since mute,
In Provence call'd, 'La belle dame sans mercy:'
Close to her ear touching the melody; –
Wherewith disturb'd, she utter'd a soft moan:
He ceased – she panted quick – and suddenly
Her blue affrayed eyes wide open shone:
Upon his knees he sank, pale as smooth-sculptured stone.

XXXIV

Her eyes were open, but she still beheld,
Now wide awake, the vision of her sleep:
There was a painful change, that nigh expell'd
The blisses of her dream so pure and deep

At which fair Madeline began to weep,
And moan forth witless words with many a sigh;
While still her gaze on Porphyro would keep;
Who knelt, with joined hands and piteous eye,
Fearing to move or speak, she look'd so dreamingly.

XXXV

'Ah, Porphyro!' said she, 'but even now
Thy voice was at sweet tremble in mine ear,
Made tuneable with every sweetest vow;
And those sad eyes were spiritual and clear:
How changed thou art! how palid, chill, and drear!
Give me that voice again, my Porphyro,
Those looks immortal, those complainings dear!
O leave me not in this eternal woe,
For if thou diest, my Love, I know not where to go.'

XXXVI

Beyond a mortal man impassion'd far
At these voluptuous accents, he arose,
Ethereal flush'd, and like a throbbing star
Seen mid the sapphire heaven's deep repose;
Into her dream he melted, as the rose
Blendeth its odour with the violet, –
Solution sweet: meantime the frost-wind blows
Like Love's alarum pattering the sharp sleet
Against the window-panes; St Agnes' moon hath set.

XXXVII

'Tis dark: quick pattereth the flaw-blown sleet:
'This is no dream, my bride, my Madeline!'
'Tis dark: the iced gusts still rave and beat:
'No dream, alas! alas! and woe is mine!
Porphyro will leave me here to fade and pine. –
Cruel! what traitor could thee hither bring?
I curse not, for my heart is lost in thine,
Though thou forsakest a deceived thing; –
A dove forlorn and lost with sick unpruned wing.'

XXXVIII

'My Madeline! sweet dreamer! lovely bride!
Say, may I be for aye thy vassal blest?
Thy beauty's shield, heart-shaped and vermeil dyed?

142

Ah, silver shrine, here will I take my rest
After so many hours of toil and quest,
A famish'd pilgrim, – saved by miracle.
Though I have found, I will not rob thy nest
Saving of thy sweet self; if thou think'st well
To trust, fair Madeline, to no rude infidel.'

XXXIX

'Hark! 'tis an elfin-storm from faery land,
Of haggard seeming, but a boon indeed:
Arise – arise! the morning is at hand; –
The bloated wassaillers will never heed: –
Let us away my love, with happy speed;
There are no ears to hear, or eyes to see, –
Drown'd all in Rhenish and the sleepy mead:
Awake! arise! my love, and fearless be,
For o'er the southern moors I have a home for thee.'

XL

She hurried at his words, beset with fears,
For there were sleeping dragons all around,
At glaring watch, perhaps, with ready spears –
Down the wide stairs a darkling way they found. –
In all the house was heard no human sound.
A chain-droop'd lamp was flickering by each door;
The arras, rich with horseman, hawk, and hound,
Flutter'd in the besieging wind's uproar;
And the long carpets rose along the gusty floor.

XLI

They glide, like phantoms, into the wide hall;
Like phantoms, to the iron porch, they glide;
Where lay the Porter, in uneasy sprawl,
With a huge empty flaggon by his side:
The wakeful bloodhound rose, and shook his hide,
But his sagacious eye an inmate owns:
By one, and one, the bolts full easy slide: –
The chains lie silent on the footworn stones; –
The key turns, and the door upon its hinges groans.

XLII

And they are gone: ay, ages long ago
These lovers fled away into the storm.
That night the Baron dreamt of many a woe,
And all his warrior-guests, with shade and form
Of witch, and demon, and large coffin worm,
Were long be-nightmared. Angela the old
Died palsy-twitch'd, with meagre face deform;
The Beadsman, after thousand aves told,
For aye un-sought for slept among his ashes cold.

Henry King
(1592–1669)

Bishop Henry King was unlucky enough to be present at the Siege and Desecration of Chichester Cathedral, at the time the Puritan faction under Sir William Waller abolished the episcopacy. In *The Sufferings of the Clergy* (1714), one John Walker describes the afflictions against thirty-eight figures of the Chichester Cathedral Chapter, although Henry King effected his escape to Surrey, via Petworth. In a commemorative sermon at the Restoration of Charles, he makes the vivid and painful recollection of witnessing a woman captain from the New Model Army parading her troops with drums beating and colours flying through the City streets. Possibly a collective memory of such a reversal of the natural order still haunts the Sussex clergy with regard to woman priests. Bishop Henry King was restored to the See in June 1660, at the Restoration of the King, an event which, legend maintains, caused the learned scholar William Oughtred, a mathematician, literally to drop dead from joy. Henry King was the son of Bishop John King, the close friend of the poet and master of his age, John Donne, and became his literary executor. From him the Cathedral inherited Donne's library, an important collection of almost a thousand books. Three hundred of these, dating from the thirteenth century to the end of the Civil Wars, are still extant in the Cathedral library, some fourteen copies identifiable as Donne's, six of them appended with his signature.

Henry enjoyed a successful ecclesiastical career, aided, one assumes, by his father's influence. John King was Bishop of London. A sermon was preached by Henry at Paul's Cross, when he was Archdeacon of Colchester. 'He did reasonably well,' commented an onlooker, 'but nothing extraordinary.' Samuel Pepys, in his diaries, refers several times to Henry King's preaching, but never with much enthusiasm.

After the barbarities at Chichester, when he suffered many indignities, including the sequestration of his estates, King lived in 'sad Retirement' during the remainder of the war, and in several moving elegies he commemorates the exiled years. These are dignified, musical, not unlike the solemn funeral music Henry Purcell wrote a little later on, for the deceased Queen Mary; but nothing is more sonorous, and even more profoundly felt than 'The Exequy' on his wife's death, in 1664, who died after a mere seven years' marriage, and about as many children. In spite of the passionate grief and controlled lament to his 'dead Saint' (an echo of John Donne), and in spite of his vow to live with but half a heart 'Till we shall meet and never part', an honourable sentiment, the reality is a little less romantic. Six years later he was addressing a second wife-to-be in lines addressed to the paradox That it is best for a Young Maid to Marry an Old Man:

> Fair one, why cannot you an old man love?
> He may as useful and as constant prove.

King begins, and he concludes:

> And you shall find, if You will choose a Man,
> Set justly for Your own Meridian,
> Though you perhaps let One and Twenty woo,
> Your elevation is for Fifty Two.

As Benedick says, the world must be peopled, although there were no children by this second marriage apparently, and nothing can remove the eloquence and subdued emotion of 'The Exequy'.

Warden John Sparrow, of All Souls, Oxford, wrote of Henry King, in 1925, that he was essentially an amateur, but that his verse possessed gravity and charm, and that 'he was an amateur with a tender heart, a tranquil mind, and a perfect sense of rhyme and rhythm, which made him at his best a poet not unworthy of the age in which he lived'.

The Exequy. To His Matchlesse
Never To Be Forgotten Freind

Accept thou Shrine of my dead Saint,
Instead of Dirges this complaint;
And for sweet flowres to crown thy hearse,
Receive a strew of weeping verse
From thy griev'd friend, whom thou might'st see
Quite melted into tears for thee.

Dear loss! since thy untimely fate
My task hath been to meditate
On thee, on thee: thou art the book,
The library whereon I look
Though almost blind. For thee (lov'd clay)
I languish out, not live the day,
Using no other exercise
But what I practise with mine eyes:
By which wet glasses I find out
How lazily time creeps about
To one that mourns: this, onely this
My exercise and bus'ness is:
So I compute the weary houres
With sighs dissolved into showres.

Nor wonder if my time go thus
Backward and most preposterous;
Thou hast benighted me, thy set
This Eve of blackness did beget,
Who was't my day, (though overcast
Before thou had'st thy Noon-tide past)
And I remember must in tears,
Thou scarce had'st seen so many years
As Day tells houres. By thy cleer Sun
My life and fortune first did run;
But thou wilt never more appear
folded within my Hemisphear,
Since both thy light and motion

Like a fled Star is fall'n and gon,
And twixt me and my soules dear wish
An earth now interposed is,
Which such a strange eclipse doth make
As ne're was read in Almanake.

  I could allow thee for a time
To darken me and my sad Clime,
Were it a month, a year, or ten,
I would thy exile live till then;
And all that space my mirth adjourn,
So thou wouldst promise to return;
And putting off thy ashy shrowd
At length disperse this sorrows cloud.

  But woe is me! the longest date
Too narrow is to calculate
These empty hopes: never shall I
Be so much blest as to descry
A glimpse of thee, till that day come
Which shall the earth to cinders doome,
And a fierce Feaver must calcine
The body of this world like thine,
(My Little World!). That fit of fire
Once off, our bodies shall aspire
To our soules bliss: then we shall rise,
And view our selves with cleerer eyes
In that calm Region, where no night
Can hide us from each others sight.

  Mean time, thou hast her, earth: much good
May my harm do thee. Since it stood
With Heavens will I might not call
Her longer mine, I give thee all
My short-liv'd right and interest
In her, whom living I lov'd best:
With a most free and bounteous grief,
I give thee what I could not keep.
Be kind to her, and prethee look

Thou write into thy Dooms-day book
Each parcell of this Rarity
Which in thy Casket shrin'd doth ly:
See that thou make thy reck'ning streight,
And yield her back again by weight;
For thou must audit on thy trust
Each graine and atome of this dust,
As thou wilt answer *Him* that lent,
Not gave thee, my dear Monument.

So close the ground, and 'bout her shade
Black curtains draw, my *Bride* is laid.

Sleep on my *Love* in thy cold bed
Never to be disquieted!
My last good night! Thou wilt not wake
Till I thy fate shall overtake:
Till age, or grief, or sickness must
Marry my body to that dust
It so much loves; and fill the room
My heart keeps empty in thy Tomb.
Stay for me there; I will not faile
To meet thee in that hollow Vale.
And think not much of my delay;
I am already on the way,
And follow thee with all the speed
Desire can make, or sorrows breed.
Each minute is a short degree,
And ev'ry houre a step towards thee.
At night when I betake to rest,
Next morn I rise neerer my West
Of life, almost by eight houres saile,
Then when sleep breath'd his drowsie gale.

Thus from the Sun my Bottom stears,
And my dayes Compass downward bears:
Nor labour I to stemme the tide
Through which to *Thee* I swiftly glide.

'Tis true, with shame and grief I yield,
Thou like the *Vann* first took'st the field,
And gotten hast the victory
In thus adventuring to dy
Before me, whose more years might crave
A just precedence in the grave.
But heark! My pulse like a soft Drum
Beats my approch, tells *Thee* I come;
And slow howere my marches be,
I shall at last sit down by *Thee*.

  The thought of this bids me go on,
And wait my dissolution
With hope and comfort. *Dear* (forgive
The crime) I am content to live
Divided, with but half a heart,
Till we shall meet and never part.

Rudyard Kipling
(1865–1936)

A story is told of his boyhood, India perhaps, or the terrible months at The House of Desolation in Southsea, that Kipling, when surrounded by other children, was inclined to lower his head, windmill his arms, and hurtle himself forward in a charge, crying 'Watch out – here come Ruddy!' And there has always been an aspect of that rushing forward, head down, arms akimbo, voice upraised, quality in Kipling's verses, his polemical prose, and point of view. Not everybody responds to his headlong attack. There are a number who resist it.

There were fallings out with locals when Rudyard and Carrie Kipling moved from Rottingdean in 1902, as well as frustration with tourist intrusion, and sadness at the death of their beloved daughter Josephine. They drove westward, keeping in the country. As soon as they came across Batemans, in the glorious valley below Burwash, in the northern edge of Sussex, they wanted to make their home there, responding to the favourable 'feng-shui' of the place. In the winter months the Jacobean stone house has a gloomy and austere face, almost melancholy. A visit on a summer afternoon, where long shadows extend across the lawns, and the visitor takes a gentle stroll to the farm and oast-houses, just out of sight, is an almost spiritual experience. Looking up from the fish-ponds, the visitor shares with delight the poet's masterly description of the 'blunt, bow-headed, whale-backed Downs'.

Kipling soaked himself in the Sussex atmosphere of legend, myth and fantasy, and much of it is to be discovered in the tales and poems he wrote at Batemans, in particular 'Rewards and Fairies' and 'Puck of Pook's Hill'. The point about Kipling is the gigantic size of his literary gift. Long after the so-called Imperial politics are forgotten, his magnificent short stories, children's fables, and passionate verses will be in our memories and on our lips. The silent reader, in the solitude of his armchair, should be tempted to read 'The Roman Centurion's Song' or 'The Land' or 'Sussex' out loud. He will find the presence of Ruddy in the room with him.

A Three-Part Song

I'm just in love with all these three,
The Weald and the Marsh and the Down countree.
Nor I don't know which I love the most,
The Weald or the Marsh or the white Chalk coast!

I've buried my heart in a ferny hill,
Twix' a liddle low shaw an' a great high gill.
Oh hop-bine yaller an' wood-smoke blue,
I reckon you'll keep her middling true!

I've loosed my mind for to out and run
On a Marsh that was old when Kings begun.
Oh, Romney Level and Brenzett reeds,
I reckon you know what my mind needs!

I've given my soul to the Southdown grass,
And sheep-bells tinkled where you pass.
Oh, Firle an' Ditchling an' sails at sea,
I reckon you keep my soul for me!

Rambles About Burwash
from Kipling's Sussex

I was told in the village, the house derives its name from the fact
that a grasping builder so abated his men's wages, that it was
always referred to by them as 'Batemans', and the name
endured.

from Puck of Pook's Hill

'Farewell, rewards and fairies,
Good housewives now may say,

For now foul sluts in dairies
   Do fare as well as they;
And though they sweep their hearths no less
   Than maids are wont to do,
Yet who of late for cleanliness
   Finds sixpence in her shoe?'

The Roman Centurion's Song

(Roman Occupation of Britain, A.D. 300)

Legate, I had the news last night – my cohort ordered home
By ship to Portus Itius and thence by road to Rome.
I've marched the companies aboard, the arms are stowed
   below:
Now let another take my sword. Command me not to go!

I've served in Britain forty years, from Vectis to the Wall
I have none other home than this, nor any life at all.
Last night I did not understand, but, now the hour draws near
That calls me to my native land, I feel that land is here.

Here where men say my name was made, here where my work
   was done;
Here were my dearest dead are laid – my wife – my wife and
   son;
Here where time, custom, grief and toil, age, memory, service,
   love,
Have rooted me in British soil. Ah, how can I remove?

For me this land, that sea, these airs, those folk and fields
   suffice.
What purple Southern pomp can match our changeful
   Northern skies,
Black with December snows unshed or pearled with August
   haze –

The clanging arch of steel-grey March, or June's long-lighted
   days?

You'll follow widening Rhodanus till vine and olive lean
Aslant before the sunny breeze that sweeps Nemausus clean
To Arelate's triple gate; but let me linger on,
Here where our stiff-necked British oaks confront Euroclydon!

You'll take the old Aurelian Road through shore-descending
   pines
Where, blue as any peacock's neck, the Tyrrhene Ocean shines.
You'll go where laurel crowns are won, but – will you e'er
   forget
The scent of hawthorn in the sun, or bracken in the wet?

Let me work here for Britain's sake – at any task you will –
A marsh to drain, a road to make or native troops to drill.
Some Western camp (I know the Pict) or granite Border keep,
Mid seas of heather derelict, where our old messmates sleep.

Legate, I come to you in tears – My cohort ordered home!
I've served in Britain forty years. What should I do in Rome?
Here is my heart, my soul, my mind – the only life I know.
I cannot leave it all behind. Command me not to go!

The sentiment expressed in this poem finds resonant echoes in
Edward Thomas's explanation to Eleanor Farjeon of his reason
for enlisting in World War One, and Richard Jefferies crumbling the soil of a wheat-field between his fingers.

A Charm

Take of English earth as much
As either hand may rightly clutch

In the taking of it breathe
Prayer for all who lie beneath.
Not the great nor well-bespoke,
But the mere uncounted folk
Of whose life and death is none
Report or lamentation.
Lay that earth upon thy heart,
And thy sickness shall depart!

The Land

When Julius Fabricius, Sub-Prefect of the Weald,
In the days of Diocletian owned our Lower River-field,
He called to him Hobdenius – a Briton of the Clay,
Saying: 'What about that River-piece for layin' in to hay?'

And the aged Hobden answered: 'I remember as a lad
My father told your father that she wanted dreenin' bad.
An' the more that you neeglect her the less you'll get her clean.
Have it jest *as* you've a mind to, but, if I was you, I'd dreen.'

So they drained it long and crossways in the lavish Roman
    style –
Still we find among the river-drift their flakes of ancient tile,
And in drouthy middle August, when the bones of meadows
    show,
We can trace the lines they followed sixteen hundred years ago.

Then Julius Fabricius died as even Prefects do,
And after certain centuries, Imperial Rome died too.
Then did robbers enter Britain from across the Northern main
And our Lower River-field was won by Ogier the Dane.

Well could Ogier work his war-boat – well could Ogier wield
    his brand –

Much he knew of foaming waters – not so much of farming
   land.
So he called to him a Hobden of the old unaltered blood,
Saying: 'What about that River-piece; she doesn't look no
   good?'

And that aged Hobden answered: "'Tain't for *me* to interfere,
But I've known that bit o' meadow now for five and fifty year.
Have it *jest* as you've a mind to, but I've proved it time on time,
If you want to change her nature you have *got* to give her lime!'

Ogier sent his wains to Lewes, twenty hours' solemn walk,
And drew back great abundance of the cool, grey, healing
   chalk.
And old Hobden spread it broadcast, never heeding what was
   in 't.
Which is why in cleaning ditches, now and then we find a flint.

Ogier died. His sons grew English – Anglo-Saxon was their
   name –
Till out of blossomed Normandy another pirate came;
For Duke William conquered England and divided with his
   men,
And our Lower River-field he gave to William of Warenne.

But the Brook (you know her habit) rose one rainy autumn
   night
And tore down sodden flitches of the bank to left and right.
So, said William to his Bailiff as they rode their dripping
   rounds:
'Hob, what about that River-bit – the Brook's got up no
   bounds?'

And that aged Hobden answered: "'Tain't my business to
   advise,
But ye might ha' known 'twould happen from the way the
   valley lies.
Where ye can't hold back the water you must try and save the
   sile.

Hev it jest as you've a *mind* to, but, if I was you, I'd spile!'

They spiled along the water-course with trunks of willow-trees,
And planks of elms behind 'em and immortal oaken knees.
And when the spates of Autumn whirl the gravel-beds away
You can see their faithful fragments, iron-hard in iron clay.

Georgii Quinti Anno Sexto, I, who own the River-field,
Am fortified with title-deeds, attested, signed and sealed,
Guaranteeing me, my assigns, my executors and heirs
All sorts of powers and profits which – are neither mine nor
    theirs.

I have rights of chase and warren, as my dignity requires.
I can fish – but Hobden tickles. I can shoot – but Hobden wires.
I repair, but he reopens, certain gaps which, men allege,
Have been used by every Hobden since a Hobden swapped a
    hedge.

Shall I dog his morning progress o'er the track-betraying dew?
Demand his dinner-basket into which my pheasant flew?
Confiscate his evening faggot under which my conies ran,
And summons him to judgment? I would sooner summons Pan.

His dead are in the churchyard – thirty generations laid.
Their names were old in history when Domesday Book was
    made;
And the passion and the piety and prowess of his line
Have seeded, rooted, fruited in some land the Law calls mine.

Not for any beast that burrows, not for any bird that flies,
Would I lose his large sound council, miss his keen amending
    eyes.
He is bailiff, woodman, wheelwright, field-surveyor, engineer,
And if flagrantly a poacher – 'tain't for me to interfere.

'Hob, what about that River-bit?' I turn to him again,
With Fabricius and Ogier and William of Warenne.

'Hev it jest as you've a mind to, *but*' – and here he takes
   command.
For whoever pays the taxes old Mus' Hobden owns the land.

Sussex, 1902

God gave all men all earth to love,
   But since our hearts are small,
Ordained for each one spot should prove
   Belovèd over all;
That, as he watched Creation's birth,
   So we, in godlike mood,
May of our love create our earth
   And see that it is good.

So one shall Baltic pines content,
   As one some Surrey glade,
Or one the palm-grove's droned lament
   Before Levuka's Trade.
Each to his choice, and I rejoice
   The lot has fallen to me
In a fair ground – in a fair ground –
   Yea, Sussex by the sea!

No tender-hearted garden crowns,
   No bosomed woods adorn
Our blunt, bow-headed, whale-backed Downs,
   But gnarled and writhen thorn –
Bare slopes where chasing shadows skim,
   And, through the gaps revealed,
Belt upon belt, the wooded, dim,
   Blue goodness of the Weald.

Clean of officious fence or hedge,
   Half-wild and wholly tame,
The wise turf cloaks the white cliff edge

As when the Romans came.
What sign of those that fought and died
   At shift of sword and sword?
The barrow and the camp abide,
   The sunlight and the sward.

Here leaps ashore the full Sou'west
   All heavy-winged with brine,
Here lies above the folded crest
   The Channel's leaden line;
And here the sea-frogs lap and cling,
   And here, each warning each,
The sheep-bells and the ship-bells ring
   Along the hidden beach.

We have no waters to delight
   Our broad and brookless vales –
Only the dewpond on the height
   Unfed, that never fails –
Whereby no tattered herbage tells
   Which way the season flies –
Only our close-bit thyme that smells
   Like dawn in Paradise.

Here through the strong and shadeless days
   The tinkling silence thrills;
Or little, lost, Down churches praise
   The Lord who made the hills:
But here the Old Gods guard their round,
   And, in her secret heart,
The heathen kingdom Wilfrid found
   Dreams, as she dwells, apart.

Though all the rest were all my share,
   With equal soul I'd see
Her nine-and-thirty sisters fair,
   Yet none more fair than she.
Choose ye your need from Thames to Tweed,
   And I will choose instead

Such lands as lie 'twixt Rake and Rye,
　　Black Down and Beachy Head.

I will go out against the sun
　　Where the rolled scarp retires,
And the Long Man of Wilmington
　　Looks naked toward the shires;
And east till doubling Rother crawls
　　To find the fickle tide,
By dry and sea-forgotten walls,
　　Our ports of stranded pride.

I will go north about the shaws
　　And the deep ghylls that breed
Huge oaks and old, the which we hold
　　No more than Sussex weed;
Or south where windy Piddinghoe's
　　Begilded dolphin veers
And red beside wide-bankèd Ouse
　　Lie down our Sussex steers.

So to the land our hearts we give
　　Till the sure magic strike,
And Memory, Use, and Love make live
　　Us and our fields alike –
That deeper than our speech and thought
　　Beyond our reason's sway,
Clay of the pit whence we were wrought
　　Yearns to its fellow-clay.

God gives all men all earth to love,
　　But since man's heart is small,
Ordains for each one spot shall prove
　　Belovèd over all,
Each to his choice, and I rejoice
　　The lot has fallen to me
In a fair ground – in a fair ground –
　　Yea, Sussex by the sea!

However partisan Kipling may sound about Sussex, and the essential Englishness of the Home Counties, it must never be forgotten that there was essentially a part of him which rebelled against England, its suffocating class-system, and climate, and which remains eternally alien.

Chant-Pagan

(English Irregular, discharged)

Me that 'ave been what I've been –
Me that 'ave gone where I've gone –
Me that 'ave seen what I've seen –
    'Ow can I ever take on
With awful old England again,
An' 'ouses both sides of the street,
And 'edges two sides of the lane,
And the parson an' gentry between,
An' touchin' my 'at when we meet –
    Me that 'ave been what I've been.

Me that 'ave watched 'arf a world
'Eave up all shiny with dew,
Kopje on kop to the sun,
An' as soon as the mist let 'em through
An' 'elios winkin' like fun –
Three sides of a ninety-mile square,
Over valleys as big as a shire –
'Are ye there? Are ye there? Are ye there?'
An' then the blind drum of our fire . . .
An' I'm rollin' 'is lawns for the Squire,
                                    Me!

Me that 'ave rode through the dark
Forty mile, often, on end,
Along the Ma'ollisberg Range,
With only the stars for my mark

An' only the night for my friend,
An' things runnin' off as you pass,
An' things jumpin' up in the grass,
An' the silence, the shine an' the size
Of the 'igh, unexpressible skies –
I am takin' some letters almost
As much as a mile to the post,
An' 'mind you come back with the
change!'

                                    Me!

I will arise an' get 'ence –
I will trek South and make sure
If it's only my fancy or not
That the sunshine of England is pale,
And the breezes of England are stale,
An' there's somethin' gone small with
the lot.
For *I* know of a sun an' a wind,
An' some plains and a mountain
be'ind,
An' some graves by a barb-wire fence,
An' a Dutchman I've fought 'oo might
give
Me a job were I ever inclined
To look in an' offsaddle an' live
Where there's neither a road nor a tree
–
But only my Maker an' me,
And I think it will kill me or cure,
So I think I will go there an' see.

                                    Me!

Philip Larkin
(1922–1985)

In January 1956, Philip Larkin and his companion, Monica
Jones, took a short holiday on the south coast, during which
time they visited Chichester Cathedral. He had just taken up
work in Hull, where he was to be the librarian (a post he held
for the next twenty-nine years with great distinction). The
result of the visit was to be one of, in the poet's own admission,
the most anthologised of all his poems, after 'Churchgoing' and
'This Be the Verse': his lines on 'An Arundel Tomb'. Later, he
informed his friend Anthony Thwaite, the poet and now,
trustee, that he never cared for the poem, because he felt he had
made a mess of it. He grumbled that he had got the hands and
gauntlets muddled up, (it is the *right*-hand gauntlet which is
'clasped empty in the other') and that it wasn't a knight in
armour of the reign of Edward III, but a Victorian mock-up.
Furthermore, an acquaintance of his visiting Chichester at a
later date had overheard a guide inform a group of visitors that
the monument to the FitzAlan family inspired a poem by the
contemporary poet, Philip Spender. The story of the figures,
much mutilated by the Puritan desecration in 1642, under
Colonel Waller, is explained in great and fascinating detail in
one of the Otter Memorial Papers, which examines the poems
and the monument together.

Philip Larkin was a professed atheist, and his biographer and
friend Andrew Motion sees the poem as a moving evocation of
the struggle between time and human tenderness. At the end of
the manuscript draft, Larkin wrote, 'Love isn't stronger than
death just because statues hold hands for 600 years.' A
somewhat characteristic remark. Dr Paul Foster, editor of the
Bishop Otter Papers, has a different view. 'Man will,' he
suggests, 'seek reassurance: hope is instinctual, even if what
prompts its renewal is a "detail" on a medieval tomb, or, the
Christian Easter message of the empty tomb at Gethsemane.'
Poets are not necessarily the best interpreters of their own
work, and it is for the spectator of the Arundel monument, the

reader of Philip Larkin's magnificent poem, to make his own choice.

An Arundel Tomb

Side by side, their faces blurred,
The earl and countless lie in stone,
Their proper habits vaguely shown
As jointed armour, stiffened pleat,
And that faint hint of the absurd –
The little dogs under their feet.

Such plainness of the pre-baroque
Hardly involves the eye, until
It meets his left-hand gauntlet, still
Clasped empty in the other; and
One sees, with a sharp tender shock,
His hand withdrawn, holding her hand. ·

They would not think to lie so long.
Such faithfulness in effigy
Was just a detail friends would see:
A sculptor's sweet commissioned grave
Thrown off in helping to prolong
The Latin names around the base.

They would not guess how early in
Their supine stationary voyage
The air would change to soundless damage,
Turn the old tenantry away;
How soon succeeding eyes begin
To look, not read. Rigidly they

Persisted, linked, through lengths and breadths
Of time. Snow fell, undated. Light
Each summer thronged the glass. A bright

Litter of birdcalls strewed the same
Bone-riddled ground. And up the paths
The endless altered people came,

Washing at their identity.
Now, helpless in the hollow of
An unarmorial age, a trough
Of smoke in slow suspended skeins
Above their scrap of history,
Only an attitude remains:

Time has transfigured them into
Untruth. The stone fidelity
They hardly meant has come to be
Their final blazon, and to prove
Our almost-instinct almost true:
What will survive of us is love.

D. H. Lawrence
(1885–1930)

D. H. Lawrence described himself, apprehensively standing behind his desk at the Davidson Road School for twelve-year-olds, in Croydon, as 'a quivering greyhound set to mind a herd of pigs'. He enjoyed the proximity of the open downland just beyond the tidy suburbs, took strenuous walks of twenty miles or so, and in the summer of 1909 went for a long bicycle ride over the Downs to see Kipling at Rottingdean. Had he been aware of it, there is little chance the great man would have welcomed the intrusion. Driven mad by trippers coming up in droves and horse-buses from Brighton, Kipling raged against the intrusion of his privacy behind The Elms' protective flint wall. When he was forced to pull down the blind of his study window, to deter a particularly insensitive woman staring in, she was heard to remark huffily, 'How rude!' Kipling and his wife moved on to Batemans, on the East Sussex border, in the valley just below Burwash. Lawrence abandoned teaching, after he was taken up by Ford Madox Ford, married Frieda von Richtofen Weekley, and in the summer of 1915 came again to Sussex, this time to stay as a guest of Viola Meynell's in Shed Hall, in the village of Greatham, near Pulborough. Originally a series of cattle-stalls, the little cottage was charmingly converted, and still stands to the present day, much as it was. 'Beautiful, long and narrow, like the refectory of a little monastery' is how he describes it, and the months at Shed Hall, apart from his unending quarrels with Frieda and a disastrous visit by Morgan Forster (rather than stay an extra night beneath the Lawrences' roof, E. M. F. preferred to rise before his hosts, and tramp four dark miles across the frozen fields to catch the first train back to London), were generally contented. This period of pastoral repose contributed without doubt to some of the eloquent landscape writing of *The Rainbow*, on which he was engaged almost exclusively during the Greatham months, and even to its apparently optimistic ending. Christopher Fry told me that it was during the summer months, Lawrence walked over the Downs with Eleanor Farjeon, and stopped for lunch at The Hurdlemakers, in East Dean, a still unspoilt country pub at the foot of the Downs, and Christopher's own local. Lawrence also worked on much of *England, My England* (with a narrative drawn largely from the tragic life-story of several of the Meynell clan), and the long, impassioned poem, 'New Heaven and Earth', in which he imagines himself a casualty of the deepening war in Flanders. By the summer's end the new and inevitable realities hedged him in. He returned to London to face the legal prosecution of *The Rainbow*, which was suppressed in November: his rows with Frieda grew more and more turbulent, and even public; and the refuge from the war he sought in an isolated area of Cornwall at Zennor turned into catastrophe. Then, he wrote in *Kangaroo*: 'Awful years – 1916, '17, '18, '19 – the years when the damage was done.' But between January and July 1915, he felt optimistic, creative, and exhilarated: 'I have got a new birth of life since I came down here . . . Now I feel the waking up, and the thrill in my limbs, and the wind blows ripples on my blood as it rushes against this house from the sea, full of germination and quickening.' He even responded to the charms of Worthing (like Oscar Wilde, fifteen years before), writing: 'I felt like Persephone, come up from hell.'

Sussex

We have lived a few days on the seashore, with the waves banging up at us. Also over the river, beyond the ferry, there is the flat silvery world, as in the beginning, untouched: with pale sand, and very much white foam, row after row, coming from under the sky, in the silver evening: and no people, no people at all, no houses, no buildings, only a haystack on the edge of the shingle, and an old black mill. For the rest, the flat unfinished world running with foam and noise and silvery light, and a few gulls swinging like a half-born thought. It is a great thing to realise that the original world is still there – perfectly clean and

pure, many white advancing foams, and only the gulls swinging
between the sky and the shore; and in the wind the yellow sea
poppies fluttering very hard, like yellow gleams in the wind,
and the windy flourish of the seed-horns.

from New Heaven and Earth

I

And so I cross into another world
shyly and in homage linger for an invitation
from this unknown that I would trespass on.

I am very glad, and all alone in the world,
all alone, and very glad, in a new world
where I am disembarked at last.

I could cry with joy, because I am in the new world, just
    ventured in.
I could cry with joy, and quite freely, there is nobody to know.

And whosoever the unknown people of this unknown world
    may be
they will never understand my weeping for joy to be adventur-
    ing among them.
because it will still be a gesture of the old world I am making
which they will not understand, because it is quite, quite foreign
    to them.

II

I was so weary of the world,
I was so sick of it,
everything was tainted with myself,
skies, trees, flowers, birds, water,
people, houses, streets, vehicles, machines,
nations, armies, war, peace-talking,
work, recreation, governing, anarchy,
it was all tainted with myself, I knew it all to start with
because it was all myself.

When I gathered flowers, I knew it was myself plucking my own flowering.

When I went in a train, I knew it was myself travelling by my own invention.

When I heard the cannon of the war, I listened with my own ears to my own destruction.

When I saw the torn dead, I knew it was my own torn dead body.

It was all me, I had done it all in my own flesh.

To Lady Ottoline Morrell

Greatham, Pulborough, Sussex.
March 1915

My Dear Lady Ottoline, –

Today we drove to Bognor. It was strange at Bognor – a white, vague, powerful sea, with long waves falling heavily, with a crash of frosty white out of the pearly whiteness of the day, of the wide sea. And the small boats that were out in the distance heaved, and seemed to glisten shadowily. Strange the sea was, so strong. I saw a soldier on the pier, with only one leg. He was young and handsome: and strangely self-conscious, and slightly ostentatious: but confused. As yet, he does not realize anything, he is still in the shock. And he is strangely roused by the women, who seem to have a craving for him. They look at him with eyes of longing, and they want to talk to him. He was brown and strong and handsome.

It seemed to me anything might come out of that white, silent, opalescent sea; and the great icy shocks of foam were strange. I felt as if legions were marching in the mist. I cannot tell you why, but I am afraid. I am afraid of the ghosts of the dead. They seem to come marching home in legions over the white, silent sea, breaking in on us with a roar and a white iciness. Perhaps this is why I feel so afraid, I don't know. But the land beyond looked warm, with a warm, blue sky, very homely: and over the sea legions of white ghosts tramping. I was on the pier.

I cannot tell you how icy cold my heart is with fear. It is as if we were all going to die. Did I not tell you my revolution would come? It will come, God help us. The ghosts will bring it. The touch of death is very cold and horrible on us all.

D. H. Lawrence

It is the whiteness of the ghost legions that is so awful.

from New Heaven and Earth

VII

It was the flank of my wife
I touched with my hand, I clutched with my hand,
rising, new-awakened from the tomb!
It was the flank of my wife
whom I married years ago
at whose side I have lain for over a thousand nights
and all that previous while, she was I, she was I;
I touched her, it was I who touched and I who was touched.

Yet rising from the tomb, from the black oblivion
stretching out my hand, my hand flung like a drowned man's
    hand on a rock,
I touched her flank and knew I was carried by the current in
    death
over to the new world, and was climbing out on the shore,
risen, not to the old world, the old, changeless I, the old life,
wakened not to the old knowledge
but to a new earth, a new I, a new knowledge, a new world of
    time.

Ah no, I cannot tell you what it is, the new world.
I cannot tell you the mad, astounded rapture of its discovery.

I shall be mad with delight before I have done,
and whosoever comes after will find me in the new world
a madman in rapture.

VIII

Green streams that flow from the innermost continent of the
    new world,
what are they?
Green and illumined and travelling for ever
dissolved with the mystery of the innermost heart of the
    continent,
mystery beyond knowledge or endurance, so sumptuous
out of the well-heads of the new world. –

The other, she too has strange green eyes!
White sands and fruits unknown and perfumes that never
can blow across the dark seas to our usual world!
And land that beats with a pulse!
And valleys that draw close in love!
And strange ways where I fall into oblivion of uttermost living –
Also she who is the other has strange-mounded breasts and
    strange sheer slopes, and white levels.

Sightless and strong oblivion in utter life takes possession of
    me!
The unknown, strong current of life supreme
drowns me and sweeps me away and holds me down
to the sources of mystery, in the depths,
extinguishes there my risen resurrected life
and kindles it further at the core of utter mystery.

Greatham.

Greatham, Sussex

January 28, 1915

On the Downs . . . I opened my eyes again, and saw it was

172

daytime. And I saw the sea lifted up and shining like a blade with the sun on it. And high up, on the icy wind, an aeroplane flew towards us from the land – and the men ploughing and the boys in the fields on the table-lands, and the shepherds, stood back from their work and lifted their faces. And the aeroplane was small and high, in the thin, ice-cold wind. And the birds became silent and dashed to cover, afraid of the noise. And the aeroplane floated high out of sight. And below, on the level earth away down – were floods and stretches of snow, and I knew I was awake.

Lewes

E. V. Lucas always declared Lewes was old and grey before Brighton was even thought of. One of the finest small historic towns in England, Lewes provided a pivotal moment of history, even more than when the little group of martyrs around Richard Woodman blazed for the integrity of their faith. This was when Simon de Montfort received tokens of surrender from King Henry and his son, Edward, in May 1264, at the Mise of Lewes. A carefully preserved marble-topped table, formerly held in one of the houses belonging to the family of Anne of Cleves, was claimed to have borne the armour and weapons of the assassins of St Thomas à Becket, which, as is described elsewhere, promptly threw them off again.

Seven great and small churches stand proudly within the castle walls, and, near the altar of the mother church can be seen a square brass engraving dedicated to the relics of Thomas Twyne, a scholar, greatly beloved; as his epitaph, in Greek, testifies:

Alas, he is dead, this doctor;
Here he lies and lightly on him lies the earth.
When he passed away, Sussex sank down faint and nigh unto
death.

Lewes is still celebrated today for its noble castle, its perilous streets, and proximity to Glyndebourne, and for its gaol. Years and years ago, when I was still at school, one of my teachers, a Lewes prison visitor, showed me this two-stanza poem written by one of the inmates he had been counselling. It has never appeared before in print, and I have no recollection of writing it out myself. However, it is so compelling, I can remember it as accurately as the day I first saw the dog-eared envelope on which it was copied. Its title is self-evident, and I regard it as a perfect illustration of the classical 'primitive'. It is worthy of John Clare.

> Winter come over the wall terday,
> And druv the last dead leaf away;
> It crept into the bars above my cell,
> And made a winder of the well.
>
> It went into the prison-yard
> And made the earth all crisp and hard.
> It clambered up the wall so high,
> And hurried the ortumn down the sky.

I cannot claim that this miniature masterpiece was composed by a Sussex prisoner, but I note the traditional spelling of the famous Sussex word 'druv'.

R. Thurston Hopkins

A Visit To Lewes

It was to South Malling the four knightly murderers of Thomas
à Becket rode with whip and spur, after their dreadful deed. 'On
entering the house, they threw off their arms and trappings on
the large dining-table which stood in the hall, and after supper
gathered round the blazing hearth; suddenly the table started
back, and threw its burden on the ground. The attendants,
roused by the crash, rushed in with lights and replaced the
arms. But soon a second still louder crash was heard, and the
various articles were thrown still further off. Soldiers and
servants with torches searched in vain under the solid table to
find the cause of its convulsions, till one of the conscience-
stricken knights suggested that it was indignantly refusing to
bear the sacrilegious burden of their arms.' So ran the popular
story; and as late as the fourteenth century it was still shewn in
the same place – the earliest and most memorable instance of a
"rapping", "leaping" and "turning" table.

G. D. Martineau

This melancholy downland poem invites many questions on the identity of G. D. Martineau. When did he live and die? Is G. D. male or female? Above all, are there other poems as natural and full of feeling as this one?

Winter Sun

White-crowned hills in the light a-gleaming,
Pinewoods dark, with an outside glow,
Glist'ning lawns with the frost flecks teeming,
Pink clouds dull with a promised snow.
O English winter, from which men run,
There's welcome cheer in your fitful sun.

Leafless bush with a straggling shadow,
Flashing drip from a bough that thaws,
Sheep that start from a broad bare meadow,
Young shrubs dead with the cold that gnaws:
Deep red are the hills, when day is done,
Where sinks the ball of the winter sun.

Yellow blur on the downs far distant,
Cradled gold of the dying day,
Darkened pasture and bells insistent,
Barking search for the foolish stray,
Grey wool tufts gathering one by one
In a cold dark land, bereft of sun.

Miscellania

Although such an idea seems unlikely in the extreme, it is nevertheless a fact that the spire of Holy Trinity at Chichester is the only cathedral in England that can be seen from the sea. Sussex is such a thin, drawn-out county with an endless snaking shore, that the Mother Church is unevenly balanced between the border of Hampshire, ten miles to the west, and the historic town of Rye, more than ninety miles to the east. Owing to this eccentricity, it is said that the inhabitants of Rye can count on five cathedrals closer to their parish than Chichester, one of them in France. These are, I assume, Arundel, Rochester, Southwark, Canterbury and Boulogne.

This letter from Sir Francis Drake to Walsingham in 1587 is not generally known: 'I assure your honour the like preparation was never heard of nor known as the King of Spain hath & daily maketh to invade England – prepare England strongly and most by sea. Stop him now, and stop him for ever. Look to the coasts of Sussex.' A house near my own, rumoured to be built from the timbers of a wrecked Spanish galleon of that same disaster is known by the original ship's name, Cartegena.

Local school-children used to call the stinging-nettle 'naughty man's plaything'. Idleness, in the past, was known to villagers as 'Old Laurence has got a hold of me'. White-thorn is called 'Cuckoo's bread and Cheese tree'. Monday after Easter is Hock Monday; the Sheermouse is a curious rodent which apparently dies if it mistakenly crosses a road trodden by man.

Unusual rustic Sussex surnames which crop up in the county archives are:

Pitchfork	Leper	Hollowbone	Padge
Slybody	Silverlock	Fidge	Backfield
Hogsflesh	Fruitnight	Rougehead	Wildgoose

Fidge and Padge spring from the pages of a novel by Charles Dickens: Silverlock and Pitchfork seem to have been mislaid from the cast list of 'The Noble Tragedy of Pyramus and Thisbe'.

Storrington folk are credited with being so simple, 'they have to look at a pond to see if it rains'.

An ancient feud between Littlehampton and Arundel school-boys survives in the gibes of 'Hampton Shivers' (referring to the ague, before the brook meadows were drained) and 'Arundel Mullets' (remembering the times when shoals of mullet used to invade the River Arun).

Leslie Norris
(1921–)

Leslie Norris is one of a small, gifted group of poets, all of whom have been invited at one time or another to work as a Visiting Fellow in Creative Writing at Bishop Otter College, in Chichester. He also taught English on the staff. He was born in Merthyr Tydfil, and has written several volumes of poetry and also short stories. He was awarded the David Higham Prize for Fiction in 1978. His affectionate relationship, both in a love of poetry and an enthusiasm for teaching the young, with the Sussex writer, Ted Walker, is perfectly expressed in 'Lunch at the Orlando'. The mutual dedication of poems between Ted Walker and Leslie Norris, as well as 'His Last Autumn' (to Andrew Young) who died in 1971, link three poets, all of whom arrived in Chichester without much thought of staying, but who resided there subsequently, and found creative fulfilment.

Barn Owl

1

Ernie Morgan found him, a small
Fur mitten inexplicably upright,
And hissing like a treble kettle
Beneath the tree he'd fallen from.
His bright eye frightened Ernie,
Who popped a rusty bucket over him
And ran for us. We kept him
In a backyard shed, perched
On the rung of a broken deck-chair,
Its canvas faded to his down's biscuit.
Men from the pits, their own childhood
Spent waste in the crippling earth,
Held him gently, brought him mice
From the wealth of our riddled tenements,
Saw that we understood his tenderness,

His tiny body under its puffed quilt,
Then left us alone. We called him Snowy.

He was never clumsy. He flew
From the first like a skilled moth,
Sifting the air with feathers,
Floating it softly to the place he wanted.
At dusk he'd stir, preen, stand
At the window-ledge, fly. It was
A catching of the heart to see him go.
Six months we kept him, saw him
Grow beautiful in a way each thought
His own knowledge. One afternoon, home
With pretended illness, I watched him
Leave. It was daylight. He lifted slowly
Over the Hughes's roof, his cream face calm,
And never came back. I saw this:
And tell it for the first time,
Having wanted to keep his mystery.

2

And would not say it now, but that
This morning, walking in Slindon woods
Before the sun, I found a barn owl
Dead in the rusty bracken.
He was not clumsy in his death,
His wings folded decently to him,
His plumes, unruffled orange,
Bore flawlessly their delicate patterning.
With a stick I turned him, not
Wishing to touch his feathery stiffness.
There was neither blood nor wound on him,
But for the savaged foot a scavenger
Had ripped. I saw the sinews.
I could have skewered them out
Like a common fowl's. Moving away
I was oppressed by him, thinking
Confusedly that down the generations
Of air this death was Snowy's

Emblematic messenger, that I should know
The meaning of it, the dead barn owl.

His Last Autumn

(for Andrew Young, 1885–1971)

He had never known such an autumn.
At his slow feet were apples
Redder than sun, and small flowers,
Their names no longer thought of,

Grew afresh in his recovered innocence.
His eyes had taken colour of the speedwell.
Looking at the sea, he felt its
Lifting pull as he dived, years deep,

Where slant light picked the rocks
With brilliants. It was the distant
Road of his boyhood we drove along
On sunny afternoons, it was the laid

Dust of his past that rose beneath
our wheels. Tranquilly the weather
Lingered, warm day after warm day.
He was dead when the cold weather came.

Last Leaves

Late last night, the moon in puddles, I walked the lane
North from my gate up to the small wood where,
Stirring and trembling from the sentient trees,
The last leaves fell. I heard them in the still air
Snap. And almost saw their sifting passage down

To join their squelching fellows on the ground,
All glory gone. I tread on the black wreck
Of the year. Well, it is over.
Here, in full arboreal summer, struck
By the squinting light, I took for a hawk
No more than a flapping pigeon. I'll not make
That mistake in valid winter. No I'll see
Each full-eyed owl stir not a breath
Of frost among the visible twigs as he pads
On air; and remember the owl's truth
For the vole, the silver frog, and the
Soft-bellied mouse, her summer breeding done.

Lunch at The Orlando

(for Ted Walker)

1

Lunch time as I leave
The building in which I work
Held up by generations
Of respectful polishing. Before me
The loud relief of students
Freed for the sunshine.
Their one wish seems to be
For a quick mediterranean tan.
Mine some beer and time slowing.

Walking through the park with the day
Alight, I see the first stub-tailed
Young swallows buttoned firm
On the perilous wires, or driving aloft
In flawless mastery of the alternative air.
Holy summer, so brief, now I fear the autumn.
The great white house gleams
That Georgian Hotham built to hold his title.
A clean hatter, Lady Jersey called him.

All playing children hold in their bouncing
Hands the sweet
Holiday bloom. It is as
A mortal ghost I make a way
Through the town, for nobody sees me.

2

Cheese rolls, ham rolls, generous
Mustard, two glasses of beer
Safely shaking on a table
Too small to shelter one's knees,
A sufficient order. We eye
With casual approval the pointed skill
Of the darts players, sneer tolerantly
At the worn drinkers too mild for words
Lapped in their gentle silences, their thoughts
Slow as fish.

But however carefully I take
This uncold liquid, I feel its lake weight
Soon enough, and its physical alchemy.
By simple pressure only, it transforms me.
Hunched in gross uneasy leisure, my new Silenic
Physique uncouth around me, I am yet
Cautious I hope in my opinions.
Before my voice becomes too loud for confidence
I offer a tempered compliment here
Or a stiff judgement, imprisoning still
Those bitter sentences that all begin if only.

If only the unceasing birds
Were even momentarily still in the still skies if only
The translation of perception
Were made unforgettably perfect in concrete words
If only the sound of the true voice
Were not lost somewhere in the distorted throat
If only the naked moment were uniquely
Recognised.

3

Well Ted, safe behind my eyes
The sentences lie locked these should have been.
What if the great lines never come; I have
The cold despair of searching for them.

We say goodbye and I heave my bay of beer
Past rows of hard brown pies on the slopping bar
Into the sunlight where shadows hard as tar
Sit in the corners, down to the sea.
The young have the sandy bloom
Of the season on them. Bands of lewd boys
Roam the sands, full of innocent knowledge.
If I were to shout here, it would be
Just another call, another call.
Gull-voice, bird voice, call of the lost sea.
My time complete, I turn away, turn back.

Clymping, Sussex

I wait on the wet beach and watch the sun
Lie in a long blood on the reflecting sand.
I feel winter in a breath. Perpetual wind
Off the sea cold as gulls pulls down
To a lean crouch the marginal
Blackthorns and the bay turns round
Into a hard field. The brittle stubble ploughs
Its last year's lines. Then heavy woods inland,
In whose dark bush the copper pheasant crows.

Alfred Noyes
(1880–1958)

For somebody, who, as far as I can discover, had little or nothing to do with Sussex in his life, 'The Sussex Sailor' is a paean of triumph and celebration. If I were not certain it was by Alfred 'Breathless hush in the close tonight' Noyes, I would have sworn it was written by Hilaire Belloc. There is great charm in 'The Bee in Church', rather like an illustration of the same period.

The Bee in Church

The nestling church at Ovingdean
  Was fragrant as a hive in May;
And there was nobody within
  To preach, or praise, or pray.

The sunlight slanted through the door,
  And through the panes of painted glass,
When I stole in, alone, once more
  To feel the ages pass.

Then, through the dim grey hush there droned
  An echoing plain-song on the air,
As if some ghostly priest intoned
  An old Gregorian there.

Saint Chrysostom could never lend
  More honey to the heavenly Spring
Than seemed to murmur and ascend
  On that invisible wing.

So small he was, I scarce could see
    My girdled brown hierophant;
But only a Franciscan bee
    In such a bass could chant.

His golden Latin rolled and boomed,
    It swayed the altar flowers anew,
Till all that hive of worship bloomed
    With dreams of sun and dew.

Ah, sweet Franciscan of the May,
    Dear chaplain of the fairy queen,
You sent a singing heart away
    That day from Ovingdean.

The Sussex Sailor

O, once by Cuckmere Haven,
    I heard a sailor sing
Of shores beyond the sunset,
    And lands of lasting spring,
Of blue lagoons and palm-trees
    And isles where all was young;
But this was ever the burden
    Of every note he sung:

O, have you seen my true love
    A-walking in that land?
Or have you seen her footprints
    Upon that shining sand?
Beneath the happy palm-trees,
    By Eden whispers fanned . . .
O, have you seen my true love
    A-walking in that land?

And, once, in San Diego,
    I heard him sing again,

Of Amberley, Rye, and Bramber,
   And Brede and Fairlight Glen:
The nestling hills of Sussex,
   The russet-roofed elfin towns,
And the skylark up in a high wind,
   Carolling over the downs.

From Warbleton to Wild Brook
   When May is white as foam,
O, have you seen my dearling
   On any hills of home?
Or have you seen her shining,
   Or only touched her hand?
O, have you seen my true love
   A-walking in that land?

And, once again, by Cowfold,
   I heard him singing low,
'Tis not the leagues of ocean
   That hide the hills I know.
The May that shines before me
   Has made a ghost of May.
The valleys that I would walk in
   Are twenty years away.

O, have you seen my true love
   A-walking in that land . . .
On hills that I remember,
   In valleys I understand,
So far beyond the sunset,
   So very close at hand, –
O, have you seen my true love
   In that immortal land?

Thomas Otway
(1652–1685)

The parish church of Trotton, at the foot of the Downs, is well-known to me, from the time I lived in the churchyard at Rogate, a few miles up the road. It was in the late 1930s, and I was the smallest sliver of a boy, but the beautiful church with its famous wall-paintings was always familiar to me, as was the local ghost story, that the church was haunted by a phantom choir boy, whom I was always hoping to hear. I was much older when a striking performance of 'Venice Observed' in London reminded me that there was a Memorial to Thomas Otway in the church, where his father had been curate in the early seventeenth century. Some of his early years were spent at Woolbeding, the same enchanting hamlet, at Easebourne, near to Midhurst, where Charlotte Smith lived in the 1780s. The *Gentleman's Magazine* of the time refers to Otway as 'the unfortunate poet', and presumably he was, abandoning himself to a fast and fashionable life, ultimately short-lived. 'He gave himself up to drinking, and like the unhappy wits of that age,' writes the chronicler, 'passed his days between rioting and fasting, ranting jollity and abject penitence; carousing one week with Lord Plymouth, and then starving for a month in low company at an alehouse.' He died aged only thirty-three.

Dr Johnson wrote of him in *Lives of the English Poets*:

> But that indigence, and its concomitants, sorrow and despondency, pressed hard upon him, has never been denied, whatever immediate cause might bring him to the grave . . .
>
> He appears, by some of his verses, to have been a zealous royalist, and had what was in those times the common reward of loyalty – he lived and died neglected.

The Poet's Complaint of His Muse

'I am a wretch of honest race;
My parents not obscure, nor high in title were:
 They left me heir to no disgrace:
 My father was (a thing now rare)
 Loyal and brave: my mother chaste and fair.
Their pledge of marriage-vows was only I;
Alone I liv'd, their much-lov'd fondled boy;
They gave me generous education high,
They strove to raise my mind, and with it grew their joy
  The sages that instructed me in Arts,
   And knowledge, oft would praise my parts,
   And cheer my parents' longing hearts.
    When I was called to a dispute,
    My fellow-pupils oft stood mute:
    Yet never envy did dis-join
Their hearts from me, nor pride distemper mine.
   Thus my first years in happiness I past,
    Nor any bitter cup did taste;
   But oh! a deadly potion came at last.

From thence sad discontent, uneasy fears,
And anxious doubts of what I had to do,
 Grew with succeeding years.
The world was wide, but whither should I go?
I, whose blossoming hopes all wither'd were,
Who'd little fortune and a deal of care!
To *Britain's* great Metropolis I stray'd,
 Where fortune's general game is play'd;
Where honesty and wit are often prais'd,
But fools and knaves are fortunate and rais'd.
My forward spirit prompted me to find
 A converse equal to my mind:
But, by raw judgment easily misled,
 (As giddy callow boys
 Are very fond of toys)
I miss'd the brave and wise, and in their stead

On every sort of vanity I fed.
Gay coxcombs, cowards, knaves, and prating fools,
Bullies, of o'ergrown bulks and little souls,
   Gamesters, half-wits and spendthrifts (such as think
   Mischievous midnight frolics bred by drink
     Are gallantry and wit,
Because of their lewd understandings fit),
   Were those wherewith two years at least I spent,
To all their fulsome follies most incorrigibly bent:
    'Till at the last, myself more to abuse,
    I grew in love with a deceitful Muse.'

Mrs Paddick

For many years I have been addicted to Mrs Paddick's column in the *West Sussex Gazette*. Every Thursday there is a reprint of one of a colourful series of articles which first came out at the end of the war. The use of dialect words is effortless and unpatronising, and these brief chronicles, week after week, give a magical and unforced glimpse into our rural past.

A Gargoyle Out of Pennywinkle

By a Sussex Woman

Mrs Paddick has a wonderful gift for arranging flowers. No matter what time of year it is there is always a vase of beautifully arranged flowers on the table in her window. This morning she had gathered the first snowdrops and I said: 'Ah, but that snow must have defeated you Mrs Paddick. You couldn't find any flowers for your vase then.'

'Yes, mum, I did: pennywinkle. When there's nothing else there's most-in-ginral some pennywinkle under the bushes, as is the only flower as'll bloom in the dark. Suppose that's why some folks calls it the graveside flower.'

'Do they Mrs Paddick? I never heard that.'

'Oh yes Mum. Some folks is froudened of their own shadow and there's many a one won't have snowdrops in the house for fear that there'll be a death. Nor they won't have any pennywinkle growing in their gay-ground. I recollect old Grannie Callow used to grow a mort of pennywinkle but then she made a ointment out of its leaves.'

'What was it good for Mrs Paddick?'

'Sores and ulsters Mum, uncommon good 'twas for stopping the itching. Did you ever hear tell of anyone eating the leaves of pennywinkle Mum?'

'No and I shouldn't like to try. I have an idea they're poisonous.'

'I dunno about that Mum. But they used to say if a husband

and wife ate pennywinkle leaves together the day they was married they'd love each other all their lives.'

'Now that sounds to me as if it meant that they'd be poisoned and so of course they loved each other all their lives,' I laughed. 'Did you ever know anyone try it, Mrs Paddick?'

'No Mum. But I've made a gargoyle out of pennywinkle leaves for sore throat and it's unaccountable good. And it's good for toothache, too.'

I went to the door and looked in the porch. 'There now,' I said, feeling annoyed. 'Annie promised to leave my newspaper as she passed and she's evidently forgotten all about it.'

'Oh Annie 'ud lose her ears if they wasn't fastened on!' said Mrs Paddick. 'I'll run along an' git it for you shall I Mum?'

West Sussex Gazette, 15 February 1945

Alexander Pope
(1688–1744)

Nothing, at first appearance, could seem more urbane than Pope's masterpiece 'The Rape of the Lock'; but it has its place in this selection, because the poem owes its inspiration to an incident that genuinely occurred at the house of Old Mr Caryl of Sussex, Squire of Harting. Tradition has it that Pope based the mock-heroic stanzas on the family feud he heard about from his host, in 1712. 'Pope's Oak Tree' is still said to exist in Ladyholt Park, although the original house has long been demolished.

from The Rape of the Lock

Canto IV.

'O wretched maid!' she spread her hands, and cry'd,
(While Hampton's echoes, 'Wretched maid!' reply'd)
'Was it for this you took such constant care
The bodkin, comb, and essence to prepare?
For this your locks in paper durance bound,
For this with tort'ring irons wreath'd around?
For this with fillets strain'd your tender head,
And bravely bore the double loads of lead?
God's! shall the ravisher display your hair,
While the Fops envy, and the Ladies stare!
Honour forbid! at whose unrivall'd shrine
Ease, pleasure, virtue, all our sex resign.
Methinks already I your tears survey,
Already hear the horrid things they say,
Already see you a degraded toast,
And all your honour in a whisper lost!
How shall I, then, your helpless fame defend?

'Twill then be infamy to seem your friend!
And shall this prize, th' inestimable prize,
Expos'd thro' crystal to the gazing eyes,
And heighten'd by the diamond's circling rays,
On that rapacious hand for ever blaze?
Sooner shall grass in Hyde-park Circus grow,
And wits take lodgings in the sound of Bow;
Sooner let earth, air, sea, to Chaos fall,
Men, monkeys, lap-dogs, parrots, perish all!'

    She said; then raging to Sir Plume repairs,
And bids her Beau demand the precious hairs:
(Sir Plume of amber snuff-box justly vain,
And the nice conduct of a clouded cane)
With earnest eyes, and round unthinking face,
He first the snuff-box open'd, then the case,
And thus broke out – 'My Lord, why, what the devil?
'Z—ds! damn the lock! 'fore Gad, you must be civil!
'Plague on't! 'tis past a jest – nay prithee, pox!
'Give her the hair' – he spoke, and rapp'd his box.

    'It grieves me much' (reply'd the Peer again)
'Who speaks so well should ever speak in vain.
But by this Lock, this sacred Lock I swear,
(Which never more shall join its parted hair;
Which never more its honours shall renew,
Clipp'd from the lovely head where late it grew)
That while my nostrils draw the vital air,
This hand, which won it, shall for ever wear.'
He spoke, and speaking, in proud triumph spread
The long-contended honours of her head.

    But Umbriel, hateful Gnome! forbears not so;
He breaks the Vial whence the sorrows flow.
Then see! the nymph in beauteous grief appears,
Her eyes half-languishing, half-drown'd in tears;
On her heav'd bosom hung her drooping head,
Which, with a sigh, she rais'd; and thus she said.
'For ever curs'd be this detested day,
Which snatch'd my best, my fav'rite curl away!
Happy! ah ten times happy had I been,
If Hampton-Court these eyes had never seen!

Yet am not I the first mistaken maid,
By love of Courts to num'rous ills betray'd.
Oh had I rather un-admir'd remain'd
In some lone isle, or distant Northern land;
Where the gilt Chariot never marks the way,
Where none learn Ombre, none e'er taste Bohea!
There kept my charms conceal'd from mortal eye,
Like roses, that in deserts bloom and die.
What mov'd my mind with youthful Lords to roam?
Oh had I stay'd, and said my pray'rs at home!
'Twas this, the morning omens seem'd to tell,
Thrice from my trembling hand the patch-box fell;
The tott'ring China shook without a wind,
Nay, Poll sat mute, and Shock was most unkind!
A Sylph too warn'd me of the threats of fate,
In mystic visions, now believ'd too late!
See the poor remnants of these slighted hairs!
My hands shall rend what ev'n thy rapine spares:
These in two sable ringlets taught to break,
Once gave new beauties to the snowy neck;
The sister-lock now sits uncouth, alone,
And in its fellow's fate foresees its own;
Uncurl'd it hangs, the fatal shears demands,
And tempts once more, thy sacrilegious hands.
Oh hadst thou, cruel! been content to seize
Hairs less in sight, or any hairs but these!'

Ezra Pound
(1885–1972)

and

William Butler Yeats
(1865–1939)

It is always extraordinary to imagine these two principal movers of modern literature, Yeats and Pound, sharing a tiny cottage on the edge of the Ashdown Forest. After an initial resistance, Pound decided Sussex air agreed with him 'quite nicely', and he lived there with his new wife, Dorothy Shakespear. Stone Cottage proved to be fruitful to both of these towering pioneers of twentieth-century literature, and Pound acted as secretary to the older poet, reading Wordsworth to him in the evenings, as Yeats' eyesight was never very strong. The two poets shared the cottage for the best part of three years, between 1913 and 1916, only departing when their dynamic artistic careers divided, Pound to America, and Yeats to London in order to pursue his own ever-increasing involvement with the Irish theatre and national politics. The landscape, the views, the gentle southern climate, in truth, had virtually no effect on the Irish poet whatsoever, who completed some of his finest work during this time, inspired uniquely by the Celtic passions of Ireland and nothing but – however, the shock-haired and red-bearded Yankee, with occasional ear-ring and large Bohemian hat in the style of Aristide Bruant, remembered in later years the placid life at Stone Cottage with nostalgia: when composing his 'Pisan Cantos', while temporarily held imprisoned after the war by the Americans for his outlandish and dotty fascist views, he wrote of 'Uncle William' Yeats in affectionate lines:

> So that I recalled the noise in the chimney
> As it were, the wind in the chimney
> but was in reality Uncle William

> downstairs composing
> at Stone Cottage in Sussex by the waste moor
> (or whatever) and the holly bush
> who would not eat ham for dinner
> despite the excellent quality
> and the pleasure of having it hot . . .
> Well those days are gone forever.

After being confined to a mental institution for a further eleven years, Pound eventually returned to Rapallo, where he remained, virtually taciturn, until his death in 1972. Stone Cottage is still there, just beside a footpath, which leads from the main road onto the waste moor – the holly bush also, remains in the back garden.

Some Sussex Proverbs

> The people of Fletching
> Live by snapping and ketching.

> Proud Petworth; poor people:
> High church; crooked steeple.

Burn a Sussex man for a fool, but walk wide of his ashes!

Puritan Names

Some of the oddest of the composite names that broke out over England during the Puritan revolution are to be found in Sussex registers. In 1632, Master Performe-thy-vowes Seers of Maresfield married Thomasine Edwards. His full name was too much for the village, and four years later is found an entry recording the burial of 'Vowes Seers' pure and simple. Heathfield had many Puritan names, among them 'Replenished', which was given to the daughter of Robert Pryor in 1600. There was also a Heathfield damsel known as 'More-Fruits'. Mr Lower prints the following names from a Sussex jury list in the seventeenth century:

> Redeemed Compton of Battel
> Stand-fast-on-high Stringer of Crowhurst
> Weep-not Billing of Lewes
> Called Lower of Warbleton
> Elected Mitchell of Heathfield
> Renewed Wisberry of Hailsham
> Fly-fornication Richardson of Waldron
> The-Peace-of-God Knight of Burwash
> Fight-the-good-fight-of-faith White of Ewhurst
> Kill-sin Pemble of Withyham

Also a Master More-Fruits Fowler of East Hoathly, for it seems that in such names there was no sex.

Rottingdean boys, Rottingdean boys, eyes like diamonds, teeth like pearls,
   Laced up boots and corduroys, you cannot better those Rottingdean boys.

Inscriptions on Rye Bells

To honour both of God and King
Our voices shall in concert ring.

May heaven increase their bounteous store
And bless their souls for evermore.

Whilst thus we join in joyful sound
May love and loyalty abound.

Ye people all who hear me ring
Be faithful to your God and King.

Such wondrous power to music's given
It elevates the soul to heaven.

If you have a judicious ear
You'll own my voice is sweet and clear.

Our voices shall with joyful sound
Make hills and valleys echo round.

In wedlock bands all ye who join,
With hands your hearts unite;
So shall our tuneful tongues combine
To laud the nuptial rite.

Ye ringers, all who prize
Your health and happiness,
Be sober, merry, wise,
And you'll the same possess.

Charles Sackville

Charles Sackville, sixth Earl of Dorset, One of the rakish friends of Charles II, had little to commend him in his younger days. Even Samuel Pepys found him rather shocking. He had the facility of writing attractive, light-hearted verses, typical of which are the following lines. Dr Johnson, the Great Cham of English Literature, described the Earl's verses as 'gay, vigorous and airy'. The Sackvilles came originally from Buckhurst in north Sussex.

To All The Ladies Now On Land

To all you ladies now on land,
We men at sea indite;
But first would have you understand
How hard it is to write;
The Muses now, and Neptune too,
We must implore to write to you.

For though the Muses should prove kind,
And fill our empty brain;
Yet if rough Neptune rouse the wind,
To wave the azure main,
Our paper, pen and ink, and we,
Roll up and down our ships at sea.

Then if we write not by each post,
Think not we are unkind;
Nor yet conclude our ships are lost
By Dutchmen or by wind;
Our tears we'll send a speedier way:
The tide shall bring them twice a day.

Percy Bysshe Shelley
(1792–1822)

Shelley.

Shelley's life is so brief that half of it appears to have been spent at Field Place, three miles from Horsham, and the family home of the Bysshe Shelleys since 1729. In reality, once the scandal erupted at Oxford of the publication of his pamphlet, 'The Necessity of Atheism' (surprisingly printed by the local Worthing firm of C. and W. Phillips), he virtually parted company with Field Place, Sussex, family, Oxford, and eventually England. This was in 1810.

Field Place, a handsome, well-proportioned manor-house, surrounded by substantial grounds, and a lake – on which the young Percy rowed a small boat, while his father, Sir Timothy blazed away at the mallards – represented a kind of idyllic childhood.

Years later, in 1816, Shelley wrote:

> Dear Home, thou scene of earliest hopes and joys,
> The least of which wronged Memory ever makes
> Bitterer than thine unremembered tears.

Shelley, ever precocious, held his audience of four younger sisters, Elizabeth, Mary, Margaret, and Hellen, enraptured and adoring, with tales of marvellous adventures. All of this joyful residence in his Sussex Eden was crudely fractured when he left, aged ten, for school at Syon House Academy, which was, according to his sympathetic cousin Tom Medwin, 'a perfect hell'. In a craving for escape, the unhappy schoolboy sketched the trees as he remembered them shading the exterior of Field Place. Eton he dreaded and hated even more, where he was bullied and humiliated and tormented beyond reason. It can fairly be said that being sent to Eton and exiled from Field Place was to the sensitive child, Shelley, every bit as traumatic as Warren's blacking-warehouse at Hungerford Stairs was to the young Charles Dickens. From his experiences at Eton he developed a passionately-held opposition of authority and contended all his life against every form of tyranny. Field Place was a refuge for him in holidays, and a return to the idealised Eden-like existence of his childhood. This lasted until the age of eighteen, when, in 1810, with the financial help of his eccentric and violent-tempered grandfather, old Bysshe, he and his sister, Elizabeth, published *Original Poetry by Victor and Cazire*, a somewhat faltering and conventional volume of Gothic verse. Phillips of Worthing were the printers, and local tradition suggests Shelley himself learnt to set up type, and spent hours in the printing office under the tuition of an attractive and intelligent young women, Miss Phillips, a relative of the two brothers. During Shelley's bicentenary year, in 1992, a plaque commemorating the site of the Phillips printing-house was erected in Warwick Street. The book can hardly be accounted a success, as there is little that is memorable in it, and the original edition of nearly 1,500 copies had to be destroyed, when the London bookseller, Stockdale, observed that Elizabeth Shelley, obviously without meaning to, had inadvertently reproduced most of a poem by the fashionable Gothic writer, Matthew 'Monk' Lewis. Before this disaster, which infuriated Shelley, a few copies had been distributed, and it was even reviewed by the *British Critic*, which assumed the anonymous author was a woman, and worse, the *Poetical Register*, which dismissed the effort entirely, concluded: 'There is no "original" poetry in this volume; there is nothing in it but downright scribble.' One piece of not altogether humourless doggerel mourns a distressed cat. Could it be the one sacrificed by the fledgling poet and scientist at Field Place, connected protestingly to an electrical kite, and flown into a thunderstorm?

After the crisis which followed publication of 'The Necessity of Atheism' (having received a threatening letter from Timothy Shelley's lawyers, can it be wondered that the luckless Phillips brothers of Worthing severed their literary association with him?), Shelley cut himself off from the rural paradise of Field Place, and all one finds in his later, great poetry, are occasional echoes or hints of a pre-Lapsarian joy. His major vision, and the ardent lyric poetry of his youthful maturity – if such a paradox may be made – exists outside nationality or even geography. Is it presumptuous to lay a claim for subconscious memories in Tuscany of larks exulting in the Sussex cornfields, and of the countryside around Horsham hovering about the Italian landscape in the 'Invitation to Jane Williams'?

Verses On a Cat

I

A cat in distress,
Nothing more, nor less;
Good folks, I must faithfully tell ye,
As I am a sinner,
It waits for some dinner
To stuff out its own little belly.

II

You would not easily guess
All the modes of distress
Which torture the tenants of earth;
And the various evils,
Which like so many devils,
Attend the poor souls from their birth.

III

Some a living require,
And others desire
An old fellow out of the way;
And which is the best
I leave to be guessed,
For I cannot pretend to say.

IV

One wants society,
Another variety,
Others a tranquil life;
Some want food,
Others, as good,
Only want a wife.

V

But this poor little cat
Only wanted a rat,

To stuff out its own little maw;
  And it were as good
  Some people had such food,
To make them *hold their jaw*!

from The Revolt of Islam
To Mary

I

So now my summer task is ended, Mary,
  And I return to thee, mine own heart's home;
As to his Queen some victor Knight of Faëry,
  Earning bright spoils for her enchanted dome;
  Nor thou disdain, that ere my fame become
A star among the stars of mortal night,
  If it indeed may cleave its natal gloom,
Its doubtful promise thus I would unite
With thy belovèd name, thou Child of love and light.

II

The toil which stole from thee so many an hour,
  Is ended, – and the fruit is at thy feet!
No longer where the woods to frame a bower
  With interlacèd branches mix and meet,
  Or where with sound like many voices sweet,
Waterfalls leap among wild islands green,
  Which framed for my lone boat a lone retreat
Of moss-grown trees and weeds, shall I be seen:
But beside thee, where still my heart has ever been.

III

Thoughts of great deeds were mine, dear Friend, when first
  The clouds which wrap this world from youth did pass.

I do remember well the hour which burst
  My spirit's sleep: a fresh May-dawn it was,
  When I walked forth upon the glittering grass,
And wept, I knew not why; until there rose
  From the near schoolroom, voices, that, alas!
Were but one echo from a world of woes –
The harsh and grating strife of tyrants and of foes.

IV

And then I clasped my hands and looked around –
  – But none was near to mock my streaming eyes,
Which poured their warm drops on the sunny ground –
  So, without shame, I spake: – 'I will be wise,
  And just, and free, and mild, if in me lies
Such power, for I grow weary to behold
  The selfish and the strong still tyrannise
Without reproach or check.' I then controlled
My tears, my heart grew calm, and I was meek and bold.

V

And from that hour did I with earnest thought
  Heap knowledge from forbidden mines of lore,
Yet nothing that my tyrants knew or taught
  I cared to learn, but from that secret store
  Wrought linkèd armour for my soul, before
It might walk forth to war among mankind;
  Thus power and hope were strengthened more and more
Within me, till there came upon my mind
A sense of loneliness, a thirst with which I pined.

VI

Alas, that love should be a blight and snare
  To those who seek all sympathies in one –
Such once I sought in vain; then black despair,
  The shadow of a starless night, was thrown
  Over the world in which I moved alone: –
Yet never found I one not false to me,
  Hard hearts, and cold, like weights of icy stone
Which crushed and withered mine, that could not be
Aught but a lifeless clod, until revived by thee.

from Hymn To Intellectual Beauty

V

While yet a boy I sought for ghosts, and sped
   Through many a listening chamber, cave and ruin,
   And starlight wood, with fearful steps pursuing
Hopes of high talk with the departed dead.
I called on poisonous names with which our youth is fed;
     I was not heard – I saw them not –
     When musing deeply on the lot
Of life, at that sweet time when winds are wooing
     All vital things that wake to bring
     News of birds and blossoming, –
     Sudden, thy shadow fell on me;
I shrieked, and clasped my hands in ecstasy!

VI

I vowed that I would dedicate my powers
     To thee and thine – have I not kept the vow?
     With beating heart and streaming eyes, even now
I call the phantoms of a thousand hours
Each from his voiceless grave: they have in visioned bowers
     Of studious zeal or love's delight
     Outwatched with me the envious night –
They know that never joy illumed my brow
     Unlinked with hope that thou wouldst free
     This world from its dark slavery,
     That thou – O awful LOVELINESS,
Wouldst give whate'er these words cannot express.

VII

The day becomes more solemn and serene
     When noon is past – there is a harmony

In autumn, and a lustre in its sky,
Which through the summer is not heard or seen,
As if it could not be, as if it had not been!
    Thus let thy power, which like the truth
    Of nature on my passive youth
Descended, to my onward life supply
    Its calm – to one who worships thee,
    And every form containing thee,
    Whom, SPIRIT fair, thy spells did bind
To fear himself, and love all human kind.

To a Skylark

Hail to thee, blithe Spirit!
    Bird thou never wert,
That from Heaven, or near it,
    Pourest thy full heart
In profuse strains of unpremeditated art.

Higher still and higher
    From the earth thou springest
Like a cloud of fire;
    The blue deep thou wingest,
And singing still dost soar, and soaring ever singest.

In the golden lightning
    Of the sunken sun,
O'er which clouds are bright'ning,
    Thou dost float and run;
Like an unbodied joy whose race is just begun.

The pale purple even
    Melts around thy flight;
Like a star of Heaven,

In the broad daylight
Thou art unseen, but yet I hear thy shrill delight,

Keen as are the arrows
Of that silver sphere,
Whose intense lamp narrows
In the white dawn clear
Until we hardly see – we feel that it is there.

All the earth and air
With thy voice is loud,
As, when night is bare,
From one lonely cloud
The moon rains out her beams, and Heaven is over-
flowed.

We look before and after,
And pine for what is not:
Our sincerest laughter
With some pain is fraught;
Our sweetest songs are those that tell of saddest thought.

Yet if we could scorn
Hate, and pride, and fear;
If we were things born
Not to shed a tear,
I know not how thy joy we ever should come near.

Better than all measures
Of delightful sound,
Better than all treasures
That in books are found,
Thy skill to poet were, thou scorner of the ground!

Teach me half the gladness
That thy brain must know,
Such harmonious madness
From my lips would flow
The world should listen then – as I am listening now.

from The Invitation: To Jane Williams

Away, away, from men and towns,
To the wild wood and the Downs –
To the silent wilderness
Where the soul need not repress
Its music, lest it should not find
An echo in another's mind,
While the touch of Nature's art
Harmonizes heart to heart.

Frequently Percy Shelley looks back to his lost childhood and
demi-Eden paradise of Field Place; but the greater part of his
creative life, and his greater lyrics, were written elsewhere and
abroad. The depth of his scorn and resentment in this sonnet
make clear his motives for departure and voluntary exile.

England in 1819

An old, mad, blind, despised, and dying king,
Princes the dregs of their dull race, who flow
Through public scorn, mud from a muddy spring, –
Rulers who neither see, nor feel, nor know,
But leech-like to their fainting country cling,
Till they drop blind in blood, without a blow, –

A people starved, and stabbed, in the untilled field, –
An army which liberticide and prey
Make as a two-edged sword to all who wield, –

Golden and sanguine laws which tempt and slay, –
Religion Christless, Godless, a book sealed, –
A Senate – time's worst statute unrepealed, –

Are graves from which a glorious phantom may
Burst to illumine our tempestuous day.

Charlotte Smith
(1749–1806)

For someone living in so exquisite a house as Woolbeding, still after several centuries delightfully remote and private from the casual passer-by, Charlotte Smith wrote deeply discouraging verses. As in:

> My fate
> Nor hope nor joy illumines – Nor for me
> Return those rosy hours which here I used to see!

Imprisoned, perhaps, in her time, Charlotte Smith had much to regret. After being educated in Chichester, she was married at the immature age of fifteen by a domineering aunt to a West Indiaman, and gave birth to nine children in almost as many years. Her husband was idle and feckless, and after an inadequate attempt at farming, they were both committed to a debtor's prison; a Dickensian story. In her day she was immensely famous for the 'Elegiac Sonnets' she composed under the friendly patronage of William Hayley, who later came to befriend Blake. This kind of patronage which assisted Mrs Smith had the reverse effect on Blake, who found it stultifying and suffocating. In an Epigram dedicated to the Hermit of Eartham, Blake writes:

> Thy Freindship oft hath made my heart to ake:
> Do be my Enemy for Freindship's sake.

It worked better with Charlotte Smith, and her sonnets were reprinted five times in five years. She separated from her husband and retired for the rest of her life to devote herself to novels, which were greatly admired by Walter Scott and the portrait painter, George Romney. Her poetry was equally praised by Wordsworth, and he called on her in 1791, when she was then living in Brighton. But for all her success at the time – and to support an estranged husband, raise a large impecunious

212

family, and write thirty-six volumes of fiction and poetry is an immense achievement for a woman in that reactionary period – a hundred years later she was forgotten, as, alas, she is today. Her sonnet about Middleton Church has some worthy sentimental phrases, and, by a shade of unhappy irony, far from the author's intention, representative of both the graveyard and Mrs Smith's artistic reputation. Both were washed away.

Composed During a Walk on the Downs

The dark and pillowy cloud, the sallow trees,
Seem o'er the ruins of the year to mourn;
And, cold and hollow, the inconstant breeze
Sobs thro' the falling leaves and wither'd fern.
O'er the tall brow of yonder chalky bourn,
The evening shades their gather'd darkness fling,
While, by the lingering light, I scarce discern
The shrieking night-jar sail on heavy wing.

To The South Downs

Ah, hills beloved! – where once an happy child,
Your beechen shades, 'your turf, your flowers, among,'
I wove your blue-bells into garlands wild,
And woke your echoes with my artless song.
Ah! hills beloved! – your turf, your flowers, remain;
But can they peace to this sad breast restore,
For one poor moment sooth the sense of pain,
And teach a breaking heart to throb no more?
And you, Aruna! – in the vale below,
As to the sea your limpid waves you bear,

Can you one kind Lethean cup bestow,
To drink a long oblivion to my care?
Ah! no! – when all, e'en Hope's last ray is gone,
There's no oblivion – but in death alone!

The Lonely Church

Press'd by the Moon, mute arbitress of tides,
While the loud equinox its power combines,
The sea no more its swelling surge confines,
But o'er the shrinking land sublimely rides.
The wild blast, rising from the Western cave,
Drives the huge billows from their heaving bed;
Tears from their grassy tombs the village dead,
And breaks the silent sabbath of the grave!
With shells and sea-weed mingled, on the shore,
Lo! their bones whiten in the frequent wave;
But vain to them the winds and waters rave;
They hear the warring elements no more;
While I am doom'd – by life's long storm opprest,
To gaze with envy on their gloomy rest.

Horace Smith
(1779–1849)

Far more congenial, in my view, is this exhilarating panegyric on behalf of Brighton, as raffish in the Regency, as it was in Graham Greene's time, and still is today. A friend of mine, who lives there and sings its rakish praises, always claims the three great cities of the world are St Petersburg, Marrakesh, and Brighton! Horace Smith made a fortune on the Exchange and retired young, and lived part of the time in France. He was a short-term friend of Keats and Shelley, handled Shelley's affairs, and wrote a series of boring novels and consistently energetic light verse. These are some characteristic lines on a typical blood of the Brummell milieu, called Harry Dashington, possibly autobiographical:

> That is, he understood computing
> The odds at any race or match;
> Was a dead hand at pigeon-shooting:
> Could kick up rows, knock down the watch –
> Play truant and the rake at random –
> Drink – tie cravats – and drive a tandem . . .

It makes the high-spirited reader long to hear more . . .

Smith lived in a grand mansion in Hanover Square, Brighton, which is every bit as elegant today as it was in the time that he lived there. Incidentally, there has to be something favourably said of a versifier who rhymes 'million', 'undone' and 'whiten', with Pavilion, London and Brighton.

Brighton

Solvitur acris hyems grata vice veris

Now fruitful autumn lifts his sunburnt head,
    The slighted Park few cambric muslins whiten,

The dry machines revisit Ocean's bed
   And Horace quits awhile the town for Brighton.

The cit foregoes his box at Turnham Green
   To pick up health and shells with Amphitrite,
Pleasure's frail daughters trip along the Steyne,
   Led by the dame the Greeks call Aphrodite.

Phoebus, the tanner, plies his fiery trade,
   The graceful nymphs ascent Judea's ponies,
Scale the west cliff, or visit the parade,
   While poor papa in town a patient drone is.

Loose trowsers snatch the wreath from pantaloons;
   Nankeen of late were worn the sultry weather in;
But now, (so will the Prince's light dragoons,)
   White jean have triumph'd o'er their Indian brethren.

Here with choice food earth smiles and ocean yawns,
   Intent alike to please the London glutton;
This, for our breakfast proffers shrimps and prawns,
   That, for our dinner, South-down lamb and mutton.

Yet here, as elsewhere, death impartial reigns
   Visits alike the cot and the Pavilion,
And for a bribe with equal scorn disdains
   My half a crown, and Baring's half a million.

Alas! how short the span of human pride!
   Time flies, and hope's romantic schemes, are undone;
Cosweller's coach, that carries four inside,
   Waits to take back the unwilling bard to London.

Ye circulating novelists, adieu!
   Long envious cords my black portmanteau tighten:
Billiards, begone! avaunt, illegal loo!
   Farewell old Ocean's bauble, glittering Brighton.

Long shalt thou laugh thine enemies to scorn,
   Proud as Phoenicia, queen of watering places!
Boys yet unbreech'd, and virgins yet unborn,
   On thy bleak downs shall tan their blooming faces.

A. C. Swinburne
(1837–1909)

Swinburne never, so far as I can tell, lived in East or West Sussex, nor even stayed there for any length of time – but he wrote these radiant lines, confident in sprung rhythms, and buried inner-rhymes, during a visit to Shoreham and Lancing. They should be honoured.

On The South Coast

Strong as time, and as faith sublime, – clothed round with
    shadows of hopes and fears,
Nights and morrows, and joys and sorrows, alive with passion
    of prayers and tears, –
Stands the shrine that has seen decline eight hundred waxing
    and waning years.

Tower set square to the storms of air and change of season that
    glooms and glows,
Wall and roof of it tempest-proof, and equal ever to suns and
    snows,
Bright with riches of radiant niches and pillars smooth as a
    straight stem grows.

Stately stands it, the work of hands unknown of: statelier, afar
    and near,
Rise around it the heights that bound our landward gaze from
    the seaboard here;
Downs that swerve and aspire, in curve and change of heights
    that the dawn holds dear.

Dawn falls fair on the grey walls there confronting dawn, on the
    low green lea,

Lone and sweet as for fairies' feet held sacred, silent and strange
and free,
Wild and wet with its rills; but yet more fair falls dawn on the
fairer sea.

Skies fulfilled with the sundown, stilled and splendid, spread as
a flower that spreads,
Pave with rarer device and fairer than heaven's the luminous
oyster-beds,
Grass-embanked, and in square plots ranked, inlaid with gems
that the sundown sheds.

Rose-red eve on the seas that heave sinks fair as dawn when the
first ray peers;
Winds are glancing from sunbright Lancing to Shoreham,
crowned with the grace of years;
Shoreham, clad with the sunset, glad and grave with glory that
death reveres.

Sheep, Horses, Oxen

Shepherd's Toast:

If I had store
By sheep and fold
I'd give you gold.
But since I'm poor
By crook and bell
I wish you well.

Heavy Horses:

One white leg – buy him.
Two white legs – try him.
Three white legs – doubt him.
Four white legs – do without him.

The Ox Team on High-and-Over Hill

Lark and Gore go before
Flute and Fiddle in the middle
Turk and Tiger go behind
Broad-horn and Buttersnout pull the plough out.

Superstition

There is a superstition in the county that if a piece of black crêpe is not put round the hive after a death in the family, the bees will die.

Alfred Lord Tennyson
(1809–1892)

Lord Tennyson

The view from Blackdown, high above Lurgashall, looks down at the groves of Aldworth, half the Weald of Sussex, over the fields where Shelley heard the skylark, from Leith Hill in Surrey to the heights of Chanctonbury Ring, and beyond the mouth of the River Arun, towards what Tennyson himself called, 'one grey glimpse of sea'.

This elevated spot is where the poet took his last look at the English countryside he loved, and this is where he died, and from here he took his last ride to his resting place in Westminster Abbey.

'They be going to carry him away,' said one of the aged inhabitants when the Great Man died, 'he'd a great deal better ha'bided here.' Alfred Tennyson, not unlike Kipling, fled to his Sussex refuge because he couldn't bear to be gawped at by tourists. One of the most eminent of Victorians, privately he disliked the attention, and resented his rôle as a 'public figure'. After an early residence at Warninglid, near Cuckfield, in an isolated and comfortless farmhouse, the Tennysons moved first to Twickenham, before settling at Freshwater, Isle of Wight, in their celebrated house, Farringford. Friends were always welcome, trippers in carriages were not, picking flowers from his garden, clamouring for autographs, and shaking the great man's hand. Tennyson purchased thirty-six acres of land on Blackdown for £1,400 and set about building himself a new house. It began its life as a humble cottage retreat, and ended as a substantial residence, of extravagant design outside, and within, luxury of luxuries, hot and cold running water – quite a rarity in 1869. He called the house 'Aldworth'. There he completed his narrative masterwork, *Idylls of the King*, staying there throughout the summer months to his dying day. It must be admitted in honesty, Lady Tennyson always preferred the Isle of Wight. He took strenuous walks on the steep North Downs, and across the Weald, and his eloquent musical language (described by John Betjeman as 'those long, strolling lines of his, which come from Lincolnshire, Tennyson's county, a poet's county') found its way effortlessly into the South Country as well. Aged eighty-three, he died in the autumn of 1892, at Aldworth, very peacefully, almost serene. Hallam, his son, describes the funeral procession, bedecked with wreaths of wild flowers from every county in the land: 'Ourselves, the villagers and the school children followed over the moor, through our lane towards a glorious sunset, and later through Haslemere under brilliant starlight to Westminster Abbey.' His great pet hound, alone in the empty house, apparently howled with grief.

from Idylls of the King
The Passing of Arthur

And slowly answer'd Arthur from the barge:
'The old order changeth, yielding place to new,
And God fulfils himself in many ways,
Lest one good custom should corrupt the world.
Comfort thyself: what comfort is in me?
I have lived my life, and that which I have done
May He within himself make pure! but thou,
If thou shouldst never see my face again,
Pray for my soul. More things are wrought by prayer
Than this world dreams of. Wherefore, let thy voice
Rise like a fountain for me night and day.
For what are men better than sheep or goats
That nourish a blind life within the brain,
If, knowing God, they lift not hands of prayer
Both for themselves and those who call them friend?
For so the whole round earth is every way
Bound by gold chains about the feet of God.
But now farewell. I am going a long way
With these thou seëst – if indeed I go
(For all my mind is clouded with a doubt) –
To the island-valley of Avilion;
Where falls not hail, or rain, or any snow,
Nor ever wind blows loudly; but it lies
Deep-meadow'd, happy, fair with orchard lawns

And bowery hollows crown'd with summer sea,
Where I will heal me of my grievous wound.'

So said he, and the barge with oar and sail
Moved from the brink, like some full-breasted swan
That, fluting a wild carol ere her death,
Ruffles her pure cold plume, and takes the flood
With swarthy webs. Long stood Sir Bedivere
Revolving many memories, till the hull
Look'd one black dot against the verge of dawn,
And on the mere the wailing died away.

But when that moan had past for evermore,
The stillness of the dead world's winter dawn
Amazed him, and he groan'd, 'The King is gone.'
And therewithal came on him the weird rhyme,
'From the great deep to the great deep he goes.'

Whereat he slowly turn'd and slowly clomb
The last hard footstep of that iron crag;
Thence mark'd the black hull moving yet, and cried,
'He passes to be King among the dead,
And after healing of his grievous wound
He comes again; but – if he come no more –
O me, be yon dark Queens in yon black boat,
Who shriek'd and wail'd, the three whereat we gazed
On that high day, when, clothed with living light,
They stood before his throne in silence, friends
Of Arthur, who should help him at his need?'

Then from the dawn it seem'd there came, but faint
As from beyond the limit of the world,
Like the last echo born of a great cry,
Sounds, as if some fair city were one voice
Around a king returning from his wars.

Thereat once more he moved about, and clomb
Ev'n to the highest he could climb, and saw,

Straining his eyes beneath on arch of hand,
Or thought he saw, the speck that bare the King,
Down that long water opening on the deep
Somewhere far off, pass on and on, and go
From less to less and vanish into light.
And the new sun rose bringing the new year.

Tennyson's Sussex Home

Tennyson laid the foundation stone of Aldworth on 23 April (Shakespeare's birthday) 1868: the inscription on the stone running 'Prosper thou the work of our hands, O prosper thou our handiwork.' Of the site Aubrey de Vere wrote: 'It lifted England's great poet to a height from which he could gaze on a large portion of that English land which he loved so well, see it basking in its most affluent summer beauty, and only bounded by "the inviolate sea".'

June Bracken and Heather

To —

There on the top of the down,
The wild heather round me and over me June's high blue,
When I look'd at the bracken so bright and the heather so
    brown,
I thought to myself I would offer this book to you,
This, and my love together,
To you that are seventy-seven,
With a faith as clear as the heights of the June-blue heaven,
And a fancy as summer-new
As the green of the bracken amid the gloom of the heather.

Show-Day at Battle Abbey, 1876

A Garden here – May breath and bloom of spring –
The cuckoo yonder from an English elm
Crying 'with my false egg I overwhelm
The Native nest': and fancy hears the ring
Of harness, and that deathful arrow sing,
And Saxon battle-axe clang on Norman helm.
Here rose the dragon-banner of our realm:
Here fought, here fell, our Norman-slander'd king.
O Garden blossoming out of English blood!
O strange hate-healer Time! We stroll and stare
Where might made right eight hundred years ago;
Might, right? ay good, so all things make for good –
But he and he, if soul be soul, are where
Each stands full face with all he did below.

from Becket

BECKET: Better have been
A fisherman at Bosham, my good Herbert,
Thy birth-place – the sea-creek – the petty rill
That falls into it – the green field – the gray church –
The simple lobster-basket, and the mesh –
The more or less of daily labour done –
The pretty gaping bills in the home-nest
Piping for bread – the daily want supplied –
The daily pleasure to supply it.

When I was a schoolboy, as well as devouring the *Wizard* and
Hotspur, I remember hours of delight spent lying on the floor,
chin in hand, engrossed in the pages of Arthur Mee's

Children's Encyclopedia. In later years I have often wondered who Arthur Mee actually was, whether he really existed, or whether he was simply a brand name like Hoover or Horlicks, and what became of him. Even still, Arthur Mee's sheer extent of knowledge seems to me quite daunting for one poor man's brain. At the time he seemed to me omniscient, like Merlin, or Dr Bronowski. Today, in second-hand bookshops, it is very easy – and eminently worthwhile – to pick up an old copy of Arthur Mee's edition of *The King's England* for whichever county you happen to be visiting, as there were no less than thirty-six of them published, all under A. M.'s eagle editorial eye; although, I note even *he* refers to a team of 'The Compilers', who travelled half a million miles and visited 10,000 towns and villages to produce a New Domesday Book. The volumes concerning the Home Counties are full of eccentric and imaginative anecdotes, mixed in with the obvious detail of churches and town halls to see. Greatly admired in their day by John Betjeman, I remember, however out of date they may be now, they are in a completely different sphere from more up-to-date and practical versions by Reader's Digest or the AA. How otherwise might I have ever known about the legend which informs Tennyson's sinister narrative poem, 'Rizpah'?

Phoebe Hessell is famous not only in Brighton but in military history and ancient records, for she was 108 when she died in 1821: *she saw the reigns of all the Georges.* Her extraordinary story brought her a pension from the king and a place in Tennyson's poems. In order to be near her lover she dressed as a man and served for seventeen years in the British Army, being wounded at the Battle of Fontenoy. For years she kept a stall near the gardens which Brighton calls the Steine, and she was known to everybody in the fashionable years of the town. She comes into Tennyson because without her his poem 'Rizpah' would probably not have been written. It was Phoebe Hessell who led to the conviction of a man called Rooke for highway robbery. His body hung on the gibbet high on the South Downs, and after a stormy night his poor mother would steal away in the dark, climb up the Downs to the gibbet, and pick up the fragments of the body as they fell. She buried them in Old Shoreham churchyard.

from Rizpah

Wailing, wailing, wailing, the wind over land and sea –
And Willy's voice in the wind, 'O mother, come out to me.'
Why should he call me tonight, when he knows that I cannot
    go?
For the downs are as bright as day, and the full moon stares at
    the snow.

We should be seen, my dear; they would spy us out of the town.
The loud black nights for us, and the storm rushing over the
    down,
When I cannot see my own hand, but am led by the creak of the
    chain,
And grovel and grope for my son till I find myself drenched with
    the rain.

Anything fallen again? nay – what was there left to fall?
I have taken them home, I have numbered the bones, I have
    hidden them all.
What am I saying? what are *you*? do you come as a spy?
Falls? what falls? who knows? As the tree falls so must it lie.

Ah – you, that have lived so soft, what should *you* know of the
    night,
The blast and the burning shame and the bitter frost and the
    fright?
I have done it, while you were asleep – you were only made for
    the day.
I have gather'd my baby together – and now you may go your
    way.

Flesh of my flesh was gone, but bone of my bone was left –
I stole them all from the lawyers – and you, will you call it a
    theft? –
My baby, the bones that had suck'd me, the bones that had
    laughed and had cried –
Theirs? O no! they are mine – not theirs – they had moved in my
    side.

Do you think I was scared by the bones? I kiss'd 'em, I buried
    'em all –
I can't dig deep, I am old – in the night by the churchyard wall.
My Willy 'ill rise up whole when the trumpet of judgment 'ill
    sound,
But I charge you never to say that I laid him in holy ground.

The View From Blackdown Forest

Our birches yellowing and from each
    The light leaf falling fast,
While squirrels from our fiery beech
    Were bearing off the mast,
You came, and look'd and loved the view
    Long-known and loved by me,
Green Sussex fading into blue
    With one gray glimpse of sea.

Edward Thomas
(1878–1917)

It is an unashamed confession to admit that Edward Thomas is being dragged into this selection sideways, because although he is eminently a celebrant of The South Country, which was the title of one of his many books of prose, he lived principally in Hampshire – although tantalisingly a few miles on the other side of the Sussex border. This was the period of his life at Wick Green, Steep (near Petersfield), between 1908 and October 1916, when he left for training as a somewhat superannuated Officer Cadet in the Royal Artillery. Throughout this time, he took long tramps over the hills and through the woodlands of the Weald of Kent, Sussex, and Hampshire, writing his highly individual and poetic books of prose, *The South Country*, *The Icknield Way* and *In Pursuit of Spring*, all of them accounts of some kind of journeying and spiritual quest. His wife, Helen, and Gordon Bottomley, at that time were in agreement that the prose-master of *The South Country* and the emerging poet were one and the same person. Thomas felt at home in what he recognised were the Home Counties. 'Yet is this country,' he explained, 'though I am mainly Welsh, a kind of home. The people are not hospitable, but the land is.' Almost a kind of Kipling-like affirmation, some of whose values (but not others) he deeply shared. Interestingly, in his essay on Blake, 'A Literary Pilgrim in England', he disputes that the visions and inspiration Blake claims to have received from his three years at Felpham, near Bognor, were influenced in any way at all by a sense of place. 'When Blake writes about "Luvah's bulls that each morning drag the sulphur Sun out of the Deep, Harnessed with starry harness, black and shining, kept by black slaves, That work all night at the starry Harness!" these are magnificent, but they are not Sussex. They never stood outside his door at Felpham. There is no more of Felpham in it than of Hyde Park and Mile End.' If anyone would make such a condemnation of an inauthentic writer of Nature, Edward Thomas is entitled to do it! He is the most scrupulous observer of all natural things, as impeccable in his judgement and accuracy as John Clare, Gilbert White, or Richard Jefferies. His nephew, Edward Thomas who lives in Chichester, took immense pains to discover which of the works published in his *Collected Poems* in the Faber Library, 1936, related specifically to Sussex, and to help him, he asked the advice of Thomas's daughter, Myfanwy. There is obviously quite an amount describing his many walks and explorations in the county, as well as the time he lived in the Kentish Weald, when he raided the bordering county; and in his 'Literary Pilgrim in England', he recognises seven Sussex writers, including Richard Jefferies, whose biography he wrote in 1909, and W. H. Hudson, who became a good friend. Thomas's relationship with James Guthrie brings him closest to Sussex, however, and when the publisher of 'Six Poems by Edward Eastaway' produced the book in 1916, these were the first poems the young Artilleryman witnessed in print, in his own lifetime, other than two individual poems already printed in Guthrie's journal 'Root and Branch', the previous year. They first met in 1907, when Edward Thomas trudged over the Downs from Berryfield, to have tea in Guthrie's workshop in Harting. Later, when the artist, poet, and publisher moved to a tiny hamlet (now absorbed into yet more suburbs of Bognor) in Flansham, beside Blake's Felpham, the two friends, as by now they had become, met at Chichester Cross where they would smoke and drink tea and watch the to and fro of country people complete their weekend shopping. They would then walk the six or seven miles back again to Flansham, and join in sing-songs with the children around the cottage fire. James Guthrie looks back on those days as among the best he could ever remember. Edward Thomas wrote to his close friend and mentor, Robert Frost, in September, 1914, prior to his enlistment: 'I had a good ride there (to see James Guthrie at Flansham) and back over the Downs, and a swim too, in a rough cold sea rather.' Unfortunately, none of the poems first printed in Sussex contain anything which can be directly attributed to Sussex. Thomas preferred to describe country scenes and sensations, as Edward Thomas, the nephew, explains, most often in general terms, without referring to any specific place. Occasionally he describes scenes which can be directly attributed to certain areas, 'The Path', 'The Manor Farm', and several others to Steep, 'The Sheiling' to Carnforth, and uses place-names as in 'Lob' (Wiltshire), or Froxfield, Wheatham Hill and Oakshott, just over the Hampshire border, in 'Good Night'; but the only definitive Sussex place name is Chilgrove, in 'Man and Dog'. Poems like 'Roads', 'Interval', and 'The Barn', included here, have a distinctive Sussex 'feel' to them, or refer to the Weald and Downs, but these can be as well attributed to Hampshire, Surrey and especially Kent.

However, there is Myfanwy Thomas's authority for at least some authentic Sussex connections with two poems, 'The Gallows' and 'The Gypsy'. On a walk with her father, when he was staying with the Lock Ellis family at Selsfield (near East Grinstead and West Hoathly), Myfanwy definitely remembers her father pointing out to her the macabre gallows erected by the local gamekeeper, on which swung the small carcasses of crows, magpies and weasels. And she also remarks on the connection between 'The Gypsy', 'A Gentleman' and 'The Penny Whistle', and East Grinstead fair; the latter in particular, because she remembered her father seeing a gypsy boy playing such an instrument. Tenuous links, perhaps, but enough to include in this selection, one of the most striking of southland poets, who knew, in Helen, his wife's, words, 'great stretches of the South and West of England by walking: not on high roads, which he rarely used, but by forgotten ways and tracks and winding lanes. Whether he is describing a stormy sky or a ploughed field or a flower, or a movement of a stream, the reader is aware of his deep love of what he describes. . . .'

This story is well known, but has a particular resonance in this context. When his friend, the writer Eleanor Farjeon, challenged his decision to enlist, with the burning question: 'Do you know what you are fighting for?' Edward Thomas replied: 'Literally for this', and he stooped and picked up a pinch of earth and crumbled it between his fingers.

> Take of English earth as much,
> As either hand may rightly clutch,

writes Kipling in another context, but the two poets meet in expression at a similar point. Neither was as conventionally patriotic as custom assumes: least of all, Edward Thomas. He went to war to protect the spirit of England rather than her sovereignty, but if the 'Old England beautiful' was threatened, he would assert, with Coleridge,

> There lives nor form nor feeling in my soul
> Unborrowed from my country,

and he could confront no alternative option but to enlist in her defence. I make no apologies for including the piece of prose entitled quite simply 'Sussex', because it breathes like a poem, and I make no apology for including his poetry, as he exudes the living spirit of The South Country better than anybody else.

Interval

Gone the wild day:
A wilder night
Coming makes way
For brief twilight.

Where the firm soaked road
Mounts and is lost
In the high beech-wood
It shines almost.

The beeches keep
A stormy rest,
Breathing deep
Of wind from the west.

The wood is black,
With a misty steam.
Above, the cloud pack
Breaks for one gleam.

But the woodman's cot
By the ivied trees
Awakens not
To light or breeze.

It smokes aloft
Unwavering:
It hunches soft
Under storm's wing.

It has no care
For gleam or gloom:
It stays there
While I shall roam,

Die, and forget
The hill of trees,
The gleam, the wet,
This roaring peace.

The Long Small Room

The long small room that showed willows in the west
Narrowed up to the end the fireplace filled,
Although not wide. I liked it. No one guessed
What need or accident made them so build.

Only the moon, the mouse and the sparrow peeped
In from the ivy round the casement thick.
Of all they saw and heard there they shall keep
The tale for the old ivy and older brick.

When I look back I am like moon, sparrow, and mouse
That witnessed what they could never understand

Or alter or prevent in the dark house.
One thing remains the same – this my right hand

Crawling crab-like over the clean white page,
Resting awhile each morning on the pillow,
Then once more starting to crawl on towards age.
The hundred last leaves stream upon the willow.

The Penny Whistle

The new moon hangs like an ivory bugle
In the naked frosty blue;
And the ghylls of the forest, already blackened
By Winter, are blackened anew.

The brooks that cut up and increase the forest,
As if they had never known
The sun, are roaring with black hollow voices
Betwixt rage and a moan.

But still the caravan-hut by the hollies
Like a kingfisher gleams between:
Round the mossed old hearths of the charcoal-burners
First primroses ask to be seen.

The charcoal-burners are black, but their linen
Blows white on the line;
And white the letter the girl is reading
Under that crescent fine;

And her brother who hides apart in a thicket,
Slowly and surely playing
On a whistle an old nursery melody
Says far more than I am saying.

The Gallows

There was a weasel lived in the sun
With all his family,
Till a keeper shot him with his gun
And hung him up on a tree,
Where he swings in the wind and rain,
In the sun and in the snow,
Without pleasure, without pain,
On the dead oak tree bough.

There was a crow who was no sleeper,
But a thief and a murderer
Till a very late hour; and this keeper
Made him one of the things that were,
To hang and flap in rain and wind,
In the sun and in the snow.
There are no more sins to be sinned
On the dead oak tree bough.

There was a magpie, too,
Had a long tongue and a long tail;
He could both talk and do –
But what did that avail?
He, too, flaps in the wind and rain
Alongside weasel and crow,
Without pleasure, without pain,
On the dead oak tree bough.

And many other beasts
And birds, skin, bone, and feather,
Have been taken from their feasts
And hung up there together,
To swing and have endless leisure
In the sun and in the snow,
Without pain, without pleasure,
On the dead oak tree bough.

The Gypsy

A fortnight before Christmas Gypsies were everywhere:
Vans were drawn up on wastes, women trailed to the fair.
'My gentleman,' said one, 'you've got a lucky face.'
'And you've a luckier,' I thought, 'if such a grace
And impudence in rags are lucky.' 'Give a penny
For the poor baby's sake.' 'Indeed I have not any
Unless you can give change for a sovereign, my dear.'
'Then just half a pipeful of tobacco can you spare?'
I gave it. With that much victory she laughed content.
I should have given more, but off and away she went
With her baby and her pink sham flowers to rejoin
The rest before I could translate to its proper coin
Gratitude for her grace. And I paid nothing then,
As I pay nothing now with the dipping of my pen
For her brother's music when he drummed the tambourine
And stamped his feet, which made the workmen passing grin,
While his mouth-organ changed to a rascally Bacchanal dance
'Over the hills and far away.' This and his glance
Outlasted all the fair, farmer and auctioneer,
Cheap-jack, balloon-man, drover with crooked stick, and steer,
Pig, turkey, goose, and duck, Christmas corpses to be.
Not even the kneeling ox had eyes like the Romany.
That night he peopled for me the hollow wooded land,
More dark and wild than stormiest heavens, that I searched and
    scanned
Like a ghost new-arrived. The gradations of the dark
Were like an underworld of death, but for the spark
In the Gypsy boy's black eyes as he played and stamped his
    tune,
'Over the hills and far away,' and a crescent moon.

Man and Dog

"'Twill take some getting.' 'Sir, I think 'twill so.'
The old man stared up at the mistletoe
That hung too high in the poplar's crest for plunder
Of any climber, though not for kissing under:
Then he went on against the north-east wind –
Straight but lame, leaning on a staff new-skinned,
Carrying a brolly, flag-basket, and old coat, –
Towards Alton, ten miles off. And he had not
Done less from Chilgrove where he pulled up docks.
'Twere best, if he had had 'a money-box',
To have waited there till the sheep cleared a field
For what a half-week's flint-picking would yield.
His mind was running on the work he had done
Since he left Christchurch in the New Forest, one
Spring in the 'seventies, – navvying on dock and line
From Southampton to Newcastle-on-Tyne, –
In 'seventy-four a year of soldiering
With the Berkshires, – hoeing and harvesting
In half the shires where corn and couch will grow.
His sons, three sons, were fighting, but the hoe
And reap-hook he liked, or anything to do with trees.
He fell once from a poplar tall as these:
The Flying Man they called him in hospital.
'If I flew now, to another world I'd fall.'
He laughed and whistled to the small brown bitch
With spots of blue that hunted in the ditch.
Her foxy Welsh grandfather must have paired
Beneath him. He kept sheep in Wales and scared
Strangers, I will warrant, with his pearl eye
And trick of shrinking off as he were shy,
Then following close in silence for – for what?
'No rabbit, never fear, she ever got,
Yet always hunts. To-day she nearly had one:
She would and she wouldn't. 'Twas like that. The bad one.
She's not much use, but still she's company,
Though I'm not. She goes everywhere with me.

So Alton I must reach to-night somehow:
I'll get no shakedown with that bedfellow
From farmers. Many a man sleeps worse to-night
Than I shall.' 'In the trenches.' 'Yes, that's right.
But they'll be out of that – I hope they be –
This weather, marching after the enemy.'
'And so I hope. Good luck.' And there I nodded
'Good-night. You keep straight on.' Stiffly he plodded;
And at his heels the crisp leaves scurried fast,
And the leaf-coloured robin watched. They passed,
The robin till next day, the man for good,
Together in the twilight of the wood.

from The South Country

Sussex

A few miles south of that great presiding pollard beech is the
boundary line between Surrey and Kent on the north and
Sussex on the south. A few miles over the line the moorland
organ roll of heather and birch and pine succeeds the grassy
undulations and the well-grown beech and oak.

The round unending Downs are close ahead, and upon the
nearest hill a windmill beside a huge scoop in the chalk, a troop
of elms below, and then low-hedged fields of grass and wheat.
The farms are those of the downland. One stands at the end of
the elm troop that swerves and clusters about its tiled roof, grey
cliff of chimney-stack, and many gables; the stables with newer
tiles; the huge slope of the barn; the low mossy cart-lodge and
its wheels and grounded shafts; the pale straw stacks and the
dark hay ricks with leaning ladders. A hundred sheep-bells rush
by with a music of the hills in the wind. The larks are singing as
if they never could have done by nightfall. It is now the hour of
sunset, and windy. All the sky is soft and dark-grey-clouded
except where the sun, just visible and throbbing in its own light,
looks through a bright window in the west with a glow. Exactly
under the sun the grass and wheat is full both of the pure

effulgence and of the south-west wind, rippling and glittering: there is no sun for anything else save the water. North of the sun and out of its power lies a lush meadow, beyond it a flat marshland cut by several curves of bright water, above that a dark church on a wooded mound, and then three shadowy swoops of Down ending at a spire among trees.

South-west, the jagged ridgy cluster of a hillside town, a mill and a castle, stand dark and lucid, and behind them the mere lines of still more distant downs.

The Barn

They should never have built a barn there, at all –
Drip, drip, drip! – under that elm tree,
Though then it was young. Now it is old
But good, not like the barn and me.

To-morrow they cut it down. They will leave
The barn, as I shall be left, maybe.
What holds it up? 'Twould not pay to pull down.
Well, this place has no other antiquity.

No abbey or castle looks so old
As this that Job Knight built in '54,
Built to keep corn for rats and men.
Now there's fowls in the roof, pigs on the floor.

What thatch survives is dung for the grass,
The best grass on the farm. A pity the roof
Will not bear a mower to mow it. But
Only fowls have foothold enough.

Starlings used to sit there with bubbling throats
Making a spiky beard as they chattered
And whistled and kissed, with heads in air,
Till they thought of something else that mattered.

But now they cannot find a place,
Among all those holes, for a nest any more.
It's the turn of lesser things, I suppose.
Once I fancied 'twas starlings they built it for.

Francis Thompson
(1859–1907)

That strange figure, Francis Thompson, was placed under the care of the monks at Storrington Priory. Here he renounced opium for some time and his brain cleared. One might almost say that Storrington was his spiritual birthplace, for his genius, welling up in an unbroken stream, passed into 'The Ode of the Setting Sun', with its picture of the old monastery, 'The Song of Hours', and the wonderful essay on Shelley, which was thrown back on his hands by the *Dublin Review*, and which was published in that journal after his death. In 'Daisy' Storrington comes into a poem of Wordsworthian simplicity and poignancy:

> O, there were flowers in Storrington,
>   On the turf and on the spray;
> But the sweetest flower on Sussex Hills
>   Was the Daisy-flower that day!

Thompson left Storrington in February 1890 and in the next year he wrote his masterpiece, 'The Hound of Heaven', which might well stand for an echo of the spiritual fret and uneasiness of the last twenty-five years. In this poem Thompson also epitomised his own life. Whilst some men were toiling and piling up earthly treasures of one kind or another, he cared nothing for such things, and it was evident that it was his wish to remain poor. But could any better symbol of the undercurrent of the bewildered modern mind be desired than the opening stanza:

> I fled Him down the nights and down the days;
> I fled Him down the arches of the years;
> I fled him down the labyrinthine ways
> Of my own mind; and in the midst of tears
> I hid from Him and under running laughter

Up vistaed hopes, I sped;
And shot, precipitated
Adown Titanic glooms of chasmed fears,
From those strong Feet that followed, followed after.

He was 'gentle in looks, half-wild in externals, his face worn by pain and the fierce reactions of laudanum, his hair and straggling beard neglected, he had yet a distinction and an aloofness of bearing that marked him in the crowd; and when he opened his lips he spoke as a gentleman and a scholar'. His friend says: 'Unembittered, he kept his sweetness and sanity, his dewy laughter, and his fluttering gratitude. . . . I think the secret of his strength was this: that he had cast up his accounts with God and man, and thereafter stood in the mud of earth with a heart wrapped in such fire as touched Isaiah's lips.' So writes R. Thurston Hopkins in his celebration of *Kipling's Sussex*, written around 1922. Unfortunately, however, although the story of Francis Thompson's tragic life reads like the lowest depths of the decadent movement in Paris at the end of the century, the reality is that Charles-Pierre Baudelaire had completed much of his laudanum-induced poetry of spleen and damnation before Thompson was even born. The twenty-year-old Rimbaud had blazed his revolutionary poetic meteor – and destroyed it – before the Englishman had reached his teens. *Les Fleurs du Mal* and *Paradis Artificiels* were published in 1857 and 1860. Francis Thompson was born in between these two radical manifestations. *Un Saison en Enfer*, considered to be a major landmark in the history of the modern spirit, was published in 1873. Thompson was just fourteen, when Rimbaud abandoned literature. And yet, as he comes to translate his experience of opium-addiction, alcoholism and destitution, Thompson's archaic high-flown poetics are firmly rooted in the first half of the nineteenth century. His chosen language somehow fails to convince, seldom rising above a pre-Tennysonian sentimentality. It is as if the fierce experience of life at pavement level can only be expressed in the language of the conservatory. But then, Baudelaire and Rimbaud lived in Paris – not Sussex.

Daisy

Where the thistle lifts a purple crown
   Six foot out of the turf,
And the harebell shakes on the windy hill –
   O the breath of the distant surf! –

The hills look over on the South,
   And southward dreams the sea;
And, with the sea-breeze hand in hand,
   Came innocence and she.

Where 'mid the gorse the raspberry
   Red for the gatherer springs,
Two children did we stray and talk
   Wise, idle, childish things.

She listen'd with big-lipp'd surprise,
   Breast-deep 'mid flower and spine:
Her skin was like a grape, whose veins
   Run snow instead of wine.

She knew not those sweet words she spake,
   Nor knew her own sweet way;
But there's never a bird, so sweet a song
   Throng'd in whose throat that day!

O, there were flowers in Storrington
   On the turf and on the spray;
But the sweetest flower on Sussex hills
   Was the Daisy-flower that day!

Her beauty smooth'd earth's furrow'd face!
   She gave me tokens three: –
A look, a word of her winsome mouth,
   And a wild raspberry.

A berry red, a guileless look,
    A still word, – strings of sand!
And yet they made my wild, wild heart
    Fly down to her little hand.

For, standing artless as the air,
    And candid as the skies,
She took the berries with her hand,
    And the love with her sweet eyes.

The fairest things have fleetest end:
    Their scent survives their close,
But the rose's scent is bitterness
    To him that loved the rose!

She looked a little wistfully,
    Then went her sunshine way: –
The sea's eye had a mist on it,
    And the leaves fell from the day.

She went her unremembering way,
    She went, and left in me
The pang of all the partings gone,
    And partings yet to be.

She left me marvelling why my soul
    Was sad that she was glad;
At all the sadness in the sweet,
    The sweetness in the sad.

Still, still I seem'd to see her, still
    Look up with soft replies,
And take the berries with her hand,
    And the love with her lovely eyes.

Nothing begins, and nothing ends,
    That is not paid with moan;
For we are born in other's pain,
    And perish in our own.

Ode To The Setting Sun

Prelude

The wailful sweetness of the violin
　　Floats down the hushèd waters of the wind,
The heart-strings of the throbbing harp begin
　　To long in aching music. Spirit-pined,

In wafts that poignant sweetness drifts, until
　　The wounded soul ooze sadness. The red sun,
A bubble of fire, drops slowly toward the hill,
　　While one bird prattles that the day is done.

O setting Sun, that as in reverent days
　　Sinkest in music to thy smoothèd sleep,
Discrowned of homage, though yet crowned with rays,
　　Hymned not at harvest more, though reapers reap:

For thee this music wakes not. O deceived,
　　If thou hear in these thoughtless harmonies
A pious phantom of adorings reaved,
　　And echo of fair ancient flatteries!

Yet, in this field where the Cross planted reigns,
　　I know not what strange passion bows my head
To thee, whose great command upon my veins
　　Proves thee a god for me not dead, not dead!

For worship it is too incredulous,
　　For doubt – oh, too believing-passionate!
What wild divinity makes my heart thus
　　A fount of most baptismal tears? – Thy straight

Long beam lies steady on the Cross. Ah me!
　　What secret would thy radiant finger show?
Of thy bright mastership is this the key?
　　Is *this* thy secret, then? And is it woe?

Fling from thine ear the burning curls, and hark
  A song thou hast not heard in Northern day;
For Rome too daring, and for Greece too dark,
  Sweet with wild wings that pass, that pass away!

The Kingdom Of God

'In no strange land'

O world invisible, we view thee,
O world intangible, we touch thee,
O world unknowable, we know thee,
Inapprehensible, we clutch thee!

Does the fish soar to find the ocean,
The eagle plunge to find the air –
That we ask of the stars in motion
If they have rumour of thee there?

Not where the wheeling systems darken,
And our benumbed conceiving soars! –
The drift of pinions, would we hearken,
Beats at our own clay-shuttered doors.

The angels keep their ancient places; –
Turn but a stone and start a wing!
'Tis ye, 'tis your estrangèd faces,
That miss the many-splendoured thing.

But (when so sad thou canst not sadder)
Cry, – and upon thy so sore loss
Shall shine the traffic of Jacob's ladder
Pitched betwixt Heaven and Charing Cross.

Yea, in the night, my Soul, my daughter,
Cry – clinging Heaven by the hems;
And lo, Christ walking on the water
Not of Gennesareth, but Thames!

Under The Downs

There are many minute churches, standing beside yew trees
frequently as big as themselves, tucked into a cup under the
Downs, shepherd churches most of them, ministering to the
nomadic communities of the ancient past. The people come and
worship and disappear, leaving behind them no memorials, no
brass tablets, no recollection of their having ever knelt there.
One such is Didling, whose solitary bell has been ringing since
the year before the Armada, with no visible inhabitant near
enough to hear it. Two more are the twin parishes of Elsted and
Treyford, which before the war, revealed two ruined churches,
weeds round the altar, the abandoned nave congregated by
twisted trees.

An enchanting story is told of the diminutive church of
Lullington, in the Cuckmere Valley. One Sunday, in the last
century, a very small curate preached on the gospel words:
'Jesus Wept'. With only twelve people present, the collection
amounted to a modest eighteen pence. The little curate
remarked that it was the smallest church, the smallest parson,
the shortest text, the smallest congregation, and the smallest
collection he had ever heard of.

The parson of Lurgashall, Tennyson's church, had this good
piece of advice to offer:

> Those who would captivate the well-bred throng,
> Should not too often speak, nor speak too long.

Andrew Young

The Ruined Chapel

From meadows with the sheep so shorn
They, not their lambs, seem newly born
Through the graveyard I pass,
Where only blue plume-thistle waves
And headstones lie so deep in grass
They follow dead men to their graves,
And as I enter by no door
This chapel where the slow moss crawls
I wonder that so small a floor
Can have the sky for roof, mountains for walls.

Ted Walker
(1934–   )

Andrew Young always maintained that Edward Thomas was the most perfect poet writing about natural life, since John Clare. He was too modest to mention himself in the same category, but he might have done, and in the same breath, Ted Walker, who has lived and worked in Sussex for many years. He is the author of six collections of poetry, beginning in 1965 with his volume of youthful poems titled *Fox on a Barn Door*, which was welcomed as an original and striking début from a distinctive new voice. He is a Fellow of the Royal Society of Literature and writes travel books as well as short stories. More than any contemporary poet in this part of the Home Counties, Ted Walker writes topographically – in this selection, of Lancing, Bosham, Shoreham – but his images and reflections carry far more than local reverberations. He is also unique in that he is the only poet, in my view, to have written, and written well, of that remarkable footnote in Edwardian literary history, the summer visit, in August 1894, to 5 The Esplanade, Worthing, of Oscar Wilde.

Bosham

It is easy to see now,
parked at the roadside,
slow tide rising like mercury
among grasses, silvering tarmac,
how such silent encroachment
might listen to a King's word.

Across the harbour,
shingle spire corn-coloured
among red roofs
riding at anchor,

the church contains Canute's daughter.
Dust of an eight year old
in a stone coffin.

It is easy to see now
the King, his throne, the panoply
at the sea's edge,
his people trusting like children
from a safe distance,
his hands raised and the tide
declining to notice.

Yet here I could believe
I had the power,
tide on the turn.
No pause, no sense of achievement;
one second swilled to my feet
the next receding,
continuing to recede.

With it my heart goes out
to a King without choice.
Unable to stop the tide rising
nor the life of his daughter
draining too quickly.

For John Charles Walker,
Killed on Shoreham Beach

I don't think you would ever have approved
Of being in a poem. 'Mushty, look,'
I hear your spectre saying, 'keep it dark;
I wouldn't want my mates to get to know.'

But, uncle, how else can I honour you?
Time's gone when I could do the things you did.

At Cambridge I came close to what you were,
Being choked by intellectual simoom;
My most cerebral action there was the soft-
Selling of advert space in 'Cambridge Left'
To the boss of a fish-and-chip saloon.
Literally, I wore the coat you wore –

The jacket of that white alpaca suit
You dared the yobs to jeer on Worthing Prom.
My pals all wondered where I'd nicked it from
And, Brando-esque in leather, named a hand
In Poker after me. Two of a kind
I think we were in the days of that coat.

On pay-days in the shipyard you played Brag
Around an oil-drum with a greasy pack
A week's wages slipped through. You'd borrow back
Enough to stand a round of beer later.
Down the Marlipins they say you were
The sort that got offered a man's last fag.

That was before the war. Sometimes your ghost
Enters my mind, dressed in some comical
Garb; aptly in white, on a bicycle,
Fresh from a battle with lime-bags; or wet
After a fifty-foot plunge for a bet
At midnight in the Adur. It was just

Your luck to get away with it. And when
I get most sick of my gentility
And all my careful life's futility –
Pruning the bloody roses for next year,
Setting the prunings tidily on fire,
Sweeping the ashes away – why, it's then

I almost envy you that booby-trap.
All alive-o you strolled to pinch firewood
From the one innocent house that still stood
On Shoreham beach. You never knew what it meant
To look for blood in your daily excrement;
You never knew the mine that blew you up.

After the Funeral

(for William Plomer, d. September 21st 1973)

Home once more to a parched garden so sparse of flowers
It seems winter. The rose pergola bears one bud;
Here, good-humouredly, you chaffed my untidiness
Once, years back. It is hard, thinking of you as dead,

You now dumb. For the first time it is you not I
Who owe letters. I'll have, somehow, to do without
Your old-fashioned and unphonable presence who
Could be written to nights, mornings of blank despair

When no voice may be heard bearably answering back.
And, moreover, to whom now shall I send by post
Hard pears, Portuguese quinces and the home-made jams
You so savoured? Your heart stopped at the time of year

When fruit falls to the lawn harvested not by hand
But wind, cold, and a first frost that the tiring stem
Must yield to; when the great men in their severalty –
Casals, Auden, Neruda – would be taken, too.

Not young men: but their lives' work, unaccomplished quite
Lies abandoned – a spade thrust in the earth, and left.
Now my garden's a lament for the makers. Small,
Red-brown, colour of blood days old, chrysanthemums

Turn tight buds to the sun. Tendrils of summer warmth
Clasp October; the leaves cling that you saw unfurl.
Not your elegy, this, William: it's much too soon.
Come year's ending, I'll mourn not for myself, but you.

For His Old English Master

(Paul Coltman, on his retirement)

Wrought-out winter's prolonged avarice over, now
Plus June's red is a firm bargain of swollen buds;
Frost-hung meadows of fieldfares are a memory
Now one swallow suggests what is about to start.

Let's launch then into intractable metre (please
Note: accentual asclepiads), knowing your
Final term has begun ending – another spring
Too soon blown in a night-blizzard of pear-blossom.

In that garden you'd tend, under the Horse-shoe Hill,
Well you saw, with the straight eye of the countryman,
How soon after the rose aconites are in bloom.
So (since both of us loathe sentimentality)

What I'll wish for you won't be a perpetual
Leisured autumn, when your decades of retirement come.
This mid-summer, you'll take armfuls of books back home;
Some you'll read yet again, shaded by apple-trees,

And maybe – out of old habit – you'll underscore
Well-loved passages you'd have us all learn by heart.
Then, from woods that stretch far off and away, you'll hear
Crow gold pheasants, a fox bark, sense elusive lines

Lift like otter-skin, sleek pelts in the glistening
Dark. Track them: for it's mint poems I'd want for you

All your weathers to come, season by season, and
Pure, rinsed light, as of this May-time, to write them by.

Between Acts

Worthing, the nineties; pier and promenade
Busy with bathchairs, wicker bassinets.
An upper window in the Esplanade
Releases smoke of scented cigarettes.

In this lacklustre town a masterpiece
Takes shape. Elsewhere, with all the earnestness
Of being unimportant, grim police
Take evidence. So does a mad marquess.

But play, as well as The Play, must go on.
In a hired boat, and 'rented' for the day,
The author dallies down to Littlehampton.

So, bathing in fame and briny on the way,
Hubristic yet, and yet to be reviled,
Sails Oscar Fingall O'Flahertie Wills Wilde.

Mules

for Leslie Norris

In warm war sun they erupt
in frontier towns, hard-
hoofed in a dark cobbled yard,
waiting for what is apt:
cartridge cases, cordite, shells.

Always the sight of them compels
the memory of what we are.

A newsreel of a distant war
that flickers in our room recalls
a savage, wasting sense in us;

eyes that stare from skirmishes
a continent away propound
the pith of life our lives have dulled.
a braying in the silences
beyond those Asian leaves betrays

some close, restless agency,
half-detected, feared, unseen
in unfamiliar terrain,
marauding, like the lurking spy
that snipes us from the wilderness

of dreams. We know ourselves wise,
mastering violence; but sometimes,
dimly, we sense other wisdoms –
he totally lives who dies
imminently; those eyes

only that see with terror see.
We do not say we would have gone
gladly, scrabbling screes to melon-
smelling foothill towns to be
quickened with fear; nor would these

wide-eyed soldiers fail to lob
grenades at the sniper's nest
it will be time enough to test
our doctrines when our cancers throb.
But, as we watch the mules trot past,

We muse on how, in times of peace,
their withers twitch to flies
as, listlessly, they laze

neglected in corrals, or pace
at tether, shabby and unkempt.

Lancing Beach

An asphaltic sea had lain
with a rash of bladder-wrack
breaking out along its back.

It was a sea-leukaemia
and the sea convulsed with it.
throwing up silver brit

and the body of a man.
Here it was they found him, here,
with little eels in his hair,

and from his unstoppered husk
fluid flowed. Balls of black flies
rolled in the pits of his eyes.

I flung a great pearl of grief
with all my strength at the sea's
apathy. Polycrates

soon had his precious pearl back.
The rings I made would not reach
to break on that other beach:

the grief I cast was for me;
lest I lie dead on this sand.
Lie dead. In this no-man's-land.

Each stone's a necropolis.
An orthodox death. Absurd
to speak comfortable words.

The grief I cast is for me.
There is a smell of sickness –
I must come to terms with this.

Under the Pier

He has a bargain who buys
the cheap, comfortable lies
they are selling on the pier.

Inside the Hall of Mirrors
you can buy cut-price horrors:
little men with chorea

will dance for you. The Ghost Train
always brings you back again
from Hell. And you're always near

an emergency exit.
You're entitled to forget
crude facsimiles of fear –

you pay to. It's free down here
to look at the old dead-beats
who lie embalmed in their sweat

without will enough to leer
at the couples doing what
they can against the wall. Not

an urge left in them, they're
waiting till it's time to go;
they'd die, but don't know how to.

This is how things are. Nothing's
unnatural that happens.
They lie in the night and hear

the barkers up on the pier
cry dummy death for the tasting.
Down here the kicks are lasting.

Richard Williamson
(1935–   )

West Sussex is blessed in the weekly presence of Richard, son of Henry, Williamson in the pages of the *Observer*. His articles, unassuming and unfailingly apposite, appear every Thursday, shot through with perception, and wit, scholarship and poetry. Like his illustrious father – whose books on *Tarka the Otter*, *Salar the Salmon*, and other wild creatures, take us too far east or west – Richard Williamson writes firmly in the great prose tradition of Richard Jefferies and Edward Thomas. That is to say some of his articles on wild birds, the country names of flowers or fruits read like poems, which, in a sense they are. Appropriately, he is the Warden of Kingley Vale, the ancient yew-forest (the largest in England), itself the subject of frequent reference in these pages, from the fifteenth to the twentieth century, including by Gerard Young, whose essay on 'The Mysterious Weald' is reproduced below.

The Fernowl

Fernowl in night silence, fernowl in light silence,
Verge of subconscious, edge of mind dancing,
Playing in twilight, drifting through gloaming,
Finding the far edge of feeling and knowing.

When fernowl of old flighted the fern brakes,
Gliding the heather, answered by corncrakes,
Then gold flowers were closed by million in meadow
By stars flowering open undimmed by our lamp-glow.

When house talked by cowbell to house and to hamlet,
Ten thousand tin tongues in mid-summer darklit.
Came rising among them ratchet from wheelbirds
Night-calling together, ringing their strung words.

There, in that ancient, there in that simple time
The fernowl sucked with gaping mouth wide,
Hanging to teats with their feathery throats,
Keeping the devil with the milk of goats.

Gabble-ratch, litch fowl, now leaving night silent,
Fading as myths gone, going as Gods went,
Twisting and vanishing, through that dimension,
Where we once almost entered, but lost our direction.

Dwarfed by Virginia Woolf's Journal for 1941, nevertheless there is a place for three glimpses of Sussex at war. There is a touching naïvety in the poem (amateur, I suspect) from an Unknown Soldier – similarly, the rhapsody on the armada of little ships in 1940 – and, a touch of characteristic disenchantment in the poem of the Second World War.

Unknown Soldier in Flanders

Cissbury Ring

I can't forget the lane that goes from Steyning to the Ring
In summer time, and on the Down how larks and linnets sing
High in the sun. The wind comes off the sea, and, oh, the air!
I never knew till now that life in old days was so fair,
But now I know it in this filthy rat-infested ditch,
When every shell must kill or spare, and God alone knows
    which,
And I am made a beast of prey, and this trench is my lair –
My God! I never knew till now that those days were so fair.
And we assault in half-an-hour, and – it's a silly thing,
I can't forget the lane that goes from Steyning to the Ring.

Edward Shanks

The Other Little Boats

A pause came in the fighting and England held her breath,
For the battle was not ended and the ending might be death.
Then out they came, the little boats, from all the Channel
    shores:
Free men were these who hauled the ropes and sweated at the
    oars.
From Itchenor and Shoreham, from Deal and Winchelsea,
They put out into the Channel to keep their country free.

Not of Dunkirk this story, but of boatmen long ago,
When our Queen was Gloriana and King Philip was the foe,
And galleons rode the narrow seas, and Effingham and Drake
Were out of shot and powder, with all England still at stake.

They got the shot and powder, they charged the guns again,
The guns that guarded England from the galleons of Spain,
And the men that helped them do it, helped them still to hold the
    sea,
Men from Itchenor and Shoreham, men from Deal and
    Winchelsea,
Looked out happily from Heaven and cheered to see the work
Of their grandsons' grandsons' grandsons on the beaches of
    Dunkirk.

Richard Spender

Sussex Defence

In the midst of so much ugly metal,
Metal of gun and metal of mind,
We saw, and smiled at little things –
At dogs and children in the road;
At moths in tasselled grasses; at a friendly horse,
Oak-apples, tall buttercups, and pigeon cotes!

Grant me the gift that you have shown to-day,
God of all beautiful, of all strong things –
And I can see bayonets as the rushes' blades
And bullets as the rain upon a pond.
Then I shall know You in the battle,
And in the battle reach my furthest home.

Virginia Woolf
(1882–1941)

Writing to her friend Vita Sackville-West in the first year of the war, Virginia Woolf describes how she had been out walking on the marshes and discovered a swan sitting in a Saxon grave. It reminded her of Vita, she added. All her adult life, from the time she was twenty-nine – she thought of herself as unmarried, a failure, childless, insane, and no writer – Virginia Stephen found spiritual and temporal refuge in Sussex. At first in a modern ugly villa near Lewes, later on, in a handsome Victorian Gothic house at Firle, not far away. When she married Leonard they commuted from their newly founded Hogarth Press in Richmond, to Asham House, at Beddingham, and it was there that she set her ghost story, 'The Haunted House'.

Always loyal to East Sussex, the nearest she came to geographical infidelity was a suggestion that they should move to the other side of the county to Arundel, but she was persuaded against it by Leonard.

Over the years, from the profits of the Hogarth Press, the Woolfs, after the lease of Asham House ran out, purchased Monk's House in Rodmell, and set about improving its spartan disadvantages. It is difficult to imagine the pampered (in popular imagination) Bloomsberries putting up so cheerfully with outside sanitation, no bath, bats in the bedroom, mice under the bedclothes, exposed to Arctic winds, and the damp atmosphere from the marshlands of the Ouse. But they did so with a kind of zest, perhaps in contrast to the urban life of Tavistock Square.

'. . . the house is an ancient monk's house,' she wrote, 'with niches for holy water, and a great fireplace, but the best part of it is the garden. There are cherries, plums, pears, figs, together with all the vegetables. This is going to be the pride of our hearts.' And so it proved. For all her commitment to Bloomsbury values, the sophisticated London literary avant-garde, Fabianism, pacificism, the world of Lytton, Carrington, it is indisputable that Virginia Woolf found Rodmell, the surrounding countryside, and the repose of Sussex an authentic stimulation for much of her finest work, both in fiction, and in my personal view, her true masterpiece, her Journals. Tragic as it obviously appears, there is something fitting in her death in the River Ouse, behind the house. Worn out by anxieties over her own health (she heard the birds in the Sussex branches talking to one another in Greek), and depression about the impending invasion, she had asked her brother, Dr Adrian Stephen, to furnish herself and Leonard with a lethal dose of morphine, should the German army land on the south coast. She returned to the water – one of those sacred springs, perhaps referred to by Hilaire Belloc. 'I shall go down, with all my colours flying', she had confided to her diary a few days earlier. Her walking stick was found on the river bank, near to the swing-bridge between Southease and Itford, but not her body, the Ouse at that point being tidal. Schoolboys found her corpse three weeks later further down the river, on the other bank, having been returned there by a favourable tide. Her coat pockets contained pebbles with which she had weighed herself down.

Two further comments: first, the pleasing façade of Asham House exists only in old photographs now – part of that pessimistic vision Virginia Woolf shares with (ironically, as they were not compatible as artists) Hilaire Belloc and several other Sussex writers, of a vanishing rural Downland is sadly consolidated by the reality of the dreadful cement works which replaces the charming Gothic house. When I visited there three years ago only the façade remained, and notices warned that it was dangerous to approach too near for fear of falling masonry. Haunted indeed, it had the same desolation about it which afflicted Ha'nacker Mill. Second, I am aware that Virginia Woolf is not, in the exact meaning of the term, a poet. However, nobody disputes she has always written prose of a highly wrought poetic nature. For me, these astounding extracts taken from the final years of her Journals, 1940–41 capture the spirit of Sussex at war, in a manner nobody ever succeeded in doing before. They read like a continuous poem. Years before, in 1912, Virginia had arrived at Asham, newly married to Leonard. In the same month of the war, the same year, 1915 – the epoch of the Menin Road at Ypres, Suvla Bay in the Dardanelles – as Lawrence watched the white skulls of the Flanders dead emerge from the waves on Worthing beach, Virginia writes:

> Difficult to distinguish thunder from guns. German prisoners walked across the field.

In December, 1940, another year, a later war, she writes again:

> How England consoles and warms one, in these deep hollows, where the past stands almost stagnant. And the little spire across the fields. . . . So back through Lewes. And I worshipped the beauty of the country, now scraped, but with the old colours showing.

Within these profoundly moving and eloquent final entries of her Journal for 1940, Virginia Woolf writes her own epitaph, and in addition, an epitaph for the majesty of Sussex, helpless underneath the war which violated her sacred skies.

Virginia would not thank me for such a threnody, but it is truly fitting, and nearly the end of the book.

> The spring's superb adventure calls
> His dust athwart the woods to flame;
> His boundary river's secret falls
> Perpetuate and repeat his name,
> He rides the loud October sky:
> He does not die. He does not die.
>
> Belloc

Nor does Virginia.

August 1940

Tuesday 6 August

Men excavating gun emplacements in the bank. They look like little swarms of busy ants, as I walk. Cementing floors; sand bagging walls. Great lorries of material go bursting down the Roman Road. No one pays any attention – so blasé are we. Guns along the river, boughs for camouflage, excite no one. Its like the raising of the gallows tree, for an execution now expected in a week or fortnight.

Saturday 10 August

Incessant company is as bad as solitary confinement – Angelica for 2 nights, adorable, oh yes, & intimate & mature, & I see so much more of her side when I talk to her – her so reasonable & lovely side – if it werent too, a delusion. But is love ever quite a delusion? Well J.'s is. I reduce myself to initials for discretion; but can't spin a word to catch a fly after these 10 days of people & people again. Now Mabel's here wh. adds to comfort but diminishes privacy. So thats my chart at the moment. No invasion. Large air flights – little white gnats this evening. Sales very good – 2nd edition ordered. But I want sleep & silence.

Friday 16 August

Many air raids. One as I walked. A haystack was handy. But walked on, & so home. All clear. Then sirens again. Then Judith & Leslie. Bowls. All clear. Then Mrs Ebbs &c to borrow table. All clear. I must make a stop gap for the last hour, or I shall dwindle, as I'm doing here. But PH. is a concentration – a screw.

Very hot. Even out here.

(Later.) They came very close. We lay down under the tree. The sound was like someone sawing in the air just above us. We lay flat on our faces, hands behind head. Dont close yr teeth said L. They seemed to be sawing at something stationary. Bombs shook the windows of my lodge. Will it drop I asked? If so, we shall be broken together. I thought, I think, of nothingness – flatness, my mood being flat. Some fear I suppose. Shd we take Mabel to garage. Too risky to cross the garden L. said. Then another came from Newhaven. Hum & saw & buzz all round us. A horse neighed on the marsh. Very sultry. Is it thunder? I said. No guns, said L. from Ringmer, from Charleston way. Then slowly the sound lessened. Mabel in kitchen said the windows shook. Air raid still on, distant planes. Leslie playing bowls. I well beaten.

My books only gave me pain, Ch. Brontë said. Today I agree. Very heavy dull & damp. This must at once be cured. The all clear. 5 to 7. 144 down last night.

Monday 19 August
Yesterday, 18th, Sunday, there was a roar. Right on top of us they came. I looked at the plane, like a minnow at a roaring shark. Over they flashed – 3 I think. Olive green. Then pop pop pop – German? Again pop pop pop, over Kingston. Said to be 5 Bombers hedge hopping on their way to London. The closest shave so far. 144 brought down – no that was last time. And no raid (so far) today. Rehearsal. I cannot read Remorse. Why not say so?

Wednesday 28 August
How I should like to write poetry all day long – thats the gift to me of poor Ann, who never reads poetry because she hated it at school. She stayed from Tuesday to Sunday night, to be exact; & almost had me down. Why? Because (partly) she has the artists temperament without being an artist. She's temperamental, but has no outlet.

I should say, to placate V.W. when she wishes to know what was happening in Aug. 1940 – that the air raids are now at their prelude. Invasion, if it comes, must come within 3 weeks. The harrying of the public is now in full swing. The air saws; the wasps drone; the siren – its now Weeping Willie in the papers – is as punctual as the vespers. We've not had our raid yet, we say. Two in London. One caught me in the L. Library.

We went out on to the terrace, began playing. A large two decker plane came heavily & slowly – L. said a Wellesley something. A training plane said Leslie. Suddenly there was pop pop from behind the Church. Practising we said. The plane circled slowly out over the marsh & back, very close to the ground & to us. Then a whole volley of pops (like bags burst) came together. The plane swung off, slow & heavy & circling towards Lewes. We looked. Leslie saw the German black cross. All the workmen were looking. Its a German; that dawned. It was the enemy. It dipped among the fir trees over Lewes & did not rise. Then we heard the drone. Looked up & saw 2 planes very high. They made for us. We started to shelter in the Lodge. But they wheeled & Leslie saw the English sign. So we watched – they side slipped glided swooped & roared for about 5 minutes round the fallen plane as if identifying & making sure – then made off towards London. Our version is that it was a wounded plane, looking for a landing. 'It was a Jerry sure eno'' the men said: the men who are making a gun hiding by the gate. It wd have been a peaceful matter of fact death to be popped off on the terrace playing bowls this very fine cool sunny August evening.

Saturday 31 August
Now we are in the war. England is being attacked. I got this feeling for the first time completely yesterday. The feeling of pressure, danger horror. Vita rang up at 6 to say she cdn't come. She was sitting at Sissinghurst. The bombs were falling round the house. Theyd been fighting all day. I'm too jaded to give the feeling – of talking to someone who might be killed any moment. Can you hear that? she said. No, I cdnt. Thats another. That's another. She repeated the same thing – about staying in order to drive the ambulance – time after time, like a person who cant think. She'd heard that Christopher Hobhouse was killed by a bomb: that Cynthia North – so lovely like a young colt she was killed by a bomb she trod on. It was very difficult talking. She said it was a comfort to talk. She broke off – oh how I do mind this, & put the telephone down. I went & played bowls. A perfect quiet hot evening. Later the planes began zooming. Explosions. Nessa says today there was a great blaze at Ripe. A tinkling sound in the field. Bomb cases found today. A great raid on London last night. Today quiet here. The feeling is that a battle is going on – a fierce battle. May last 4 weeks. Am I afraid? Intermittently. The worst of it ones mind wont work with a spring next morning. Of course this may be the beginning of invasion. A sense of pressure. Endless local

stories. No – its no good trying to capture the feeling of England being in a battle.

Sunday 15 September

No invasion yet. Rumours that it was attempted, but barges sunk with great loss. Raids over Brighton this afternoon. Hornets (our own) swarmed over my head on the marsh. Sheep frightened. Its difficult to see the English white circle. Mabel goes tomorrow; so pray God the Church bells dont ring tonight. Now we go to our last Cook cooked dinner for I dont know how long. Could it be the end of resident servants for ever? This I pray this lovely fitful evening, as well as the usual damn Hitler prayer. Carried wood; bowls; asked for Sara Coleridge, as tho the New Statesman were immortal.

Monday 16 September

To Charleston this afternoon, after provisioning for our siege in Lewes. Last night we saw tinsel sparks here & there in the sky over the flat. L. thought they were shells bursting from the London barrage. Great air traffic all night – some loud explosions. I listened for Church Bells, thinking largely I admit, of finding ourselves prisoned here with Mabel. She thought the same. Said that if one is to be killed one will be killed. Prefers death in a Holloway shelter playing cards – naturally – to death here.

Wednesday 2 October

Ought I not to look at the sunset rather than write this? A flush of red in the blue; the haystack in the marsh catches the glow; behind me, the apples are red in the trees. L. is gathering them. Now a plume of smoke goes from the train under Caburn. And all the air a solemn stillness holds. till 8.30 when the cadaverous twanging in the sky begins; the planes going to London. Well its an hour still to that. Cows feeding. The elm tree sprinkling its little leaves against the sky. Our pear tree swagged with pears; & the weathercock above the triangular church tower above it. Why try again to make the familiar catalogue, from which something escapes. Should I think of death? Last night a great heavy plunge of bomb under the window. So near we both started. A plane had passed dropping this fruit. We went onto the terrace. Trinkets of stars sprinkled & glittering. All quiet. The bombs dropped on Itford Hill. There are two by the river, marked with white wooden crosses, still unburst. I said to L.: I dont want to die yet. The chances are against it. But theyre aiming at the railway & the power works. They get closer every time. Caburn was crowned with what looked a settled moth, wings extended – a Messerschmitt it was, shot down on Sunday.

What do I believe? Cant at the moment remember. Oh I try to imagine how one's killed by a bomb. I've got it fairly vivid – the sensation: but cant see anything but suffocating nonentity following after. I shall think – oh I wanted another 10 years – not this – & shant, for once, be able to describe it. It – I mean death; no, the scrunching & scrambling, the crushing of my bone shade in on my very active eye & brain: the process of putting out the light, – painful? Yes terrifying. I suppose so – Then a swoon; a drum; two or three gulps attempting consciousness – & then, dot dot dot

Andrew Young
(1885–1971)

Andrew Young

Leslie Norris was sharing with me, some years ago, those curious leaps of memory that link the generations backwards through the years, sometimes as far back as the nineteenth century. Generally they go, 'so and so, as a very *old* man told me, when I was a very *young* man, that he, when he was a young man, spoke to somebody who . . .', and invariably they end up at the Battle of Waterloo. But Leslie's memory leap was far and away the most engaging I have ever encountered. He told me that the poet, Canon Andrew Young, not long before his death in 1971 told him that when he was a young lad – in 1895? – his love of wild birds and natural history had been kindled by a very old man he had met after he came south from his native Scotland, who, when *he* was a young boy, had been told about these things by old John Clare, in the porch of Northampton Church, where he used to relax, chewing tobacco, when on release from the Asylum. Andrew Young had a magisterial knowledge of wild flowers, and it was said of him that he had observed every wild flower in the British Isles. He wrote about them frequently, and with scrupulous accuracy of observation, and in this, he resembles Clare more closely than any other writer, beyond Gilbert White of Selborne. But nature to him unravels his darker fears and anxieties, as well as celebrates the childlike joy of creation. A devout minister for his lifetime, although he shares the precise authenticity of other writers about the countryside (Edward Thomas immediately springs to mind), there is lurking beneath the delicate surface, sometimes as restrained and economical as Japanese haiku, the same kind of unease and anxiety which preoccupies that other minister of religion and Welsh poet, R. S. Thomas. Nameless terrors lurk, and in his later years he explored, in the poetry of *Into Hades* and its successor, life within and beyond the grave. His Sussex connections were Hove, Stonegate (near Burwash and the Kipling country), and essentially his peaceful retired life at Yapton, near Arundel. His spacious house, Park Lodge, can still be seen, and its beautiful garden, now safely tidied up since, in his final years, it grew untidy and fantastical, a sanctuary for the wild birds he cherished. His ashes were scattered over the lawns of Chichester Cathedral after his death, in his eighty-sixth year.

The Bee-Orchis

I saw a bee, I saw a flower;
I looked again and said, For sure
Never was flower, never was bee
Locked in such immobility.

The loud bees lurched about the hill,
But this flower-buried bee was still;
I said, O Love, has love the power
To change a bee into a flower.

The Flood

The winter flood is out, dully glazing the weald,
The Adur, a drowned river, lies in its bed concealed;
Fishes flowing through fences explore paddock and field.

Bushes, waist-deep in water, stand sprinkled here and there;
A solitary gate, as though hung in mid-air,
Waits idly open, leading from nowhere to nowhere.

These bushes at night-fall will have strange fish for guests,
That wagtail, tit and warbler darkened with their nests;
Where flood strays now, light-headed lapwings lifted crests.

But soon comes spring again; the hazel-boughs will angle
With bait of yellow catkins that in the loose winds dangle
And starry scarlet blossoms their blind buds bespangle;

Dogs'-mercury from the earth unfold seed-clasping fists
And green-leaved honeysuckle roll in tumbling twists
And dress of spring shake all the seeds that sleep in cists.

O blue-eyed one, too well I know you will not awake,
Who waked or lay awake so often for my sake,
Nor would I ask our last leave-taking to retake.

If lesser love of flower or bird waken my song,
It is that greater love, too full to flow along,
Falls like that Adur back, flood-like, silent and strong.

Kingley Bottom

Beneath these bine-looped yew-boughs
    Gorse blossom is outspread
Like gold that lies unguarded
    By dragons that hang dead.

All but one pterodactyl
    That hid in mist and rain
High over Kingley Bottom
    Hums like an aeroplane.

On The Pilgrims' Road

That I had hit the Road
    I partly knew
From a great Roman snail
    And sombre yew;
But that my steps went from
    And not towards
The shrine of good St Thomas,

I thought of afterwards.

So I adored to-day
   No, not his ghost,
But the saints in Westwell window,
   And her the most
Who knelt there with no head
   But was so very
Adorable a saint
   In dress of crushed strawberry.

In Moonlight

We sat where boughs waved on the ground
But made no sound;
'They cannot shake me off,'
Shrieked the black dwarf,
Impudent elf,
That was the shadow of myself.

I said to him, 'We must go now';
But from his bough
He laughed, securely perched,
'Then you rise first;'
It seemed to me
He spoke in wicked courtesy.

We rose and 'Take my hand,' he whined,
Though like the wind
Each waving bough he leapt;
And as we stept
Down the steep track
He seemed to grow more hunched and black.

Mole-Hills On The Downs

Here earth in her abundance spills
Hills on her hills,
Till every hill is overgrown
With small hills of its own;
Some old with moss and scorpion-grass,
Some new and bare and brown,
And one where I can watch the earth
Like a volcano at its birth
Still rise by falling down;
And as by these small hills I pass
And take them in my stride
I swell with pride,
Till the great hills to which I lift my eyes
Restore my size.

The Fear

How often I turn round
To face the beast that bound by bound
Leaps on me from behind,
Only to see a bough that heaves
With sudden gust of wind
Or blackbird raking withered leaves.

A dog may find me out
Or badger toss a white-lined snout;
And one day as I softly trod
Looking for nothing stranger than
A fox or stoat I met a man
And even that seemed not too odd.

And yet in any place I go
I watch and listen as all creatures do
For what I cannot see or hear,

For something warns me everywhere
That even in my land of birth
I trespass on the earth.

South Downs

No water cries among these hills,
    The mist hides and enlarges,
Though rain in every road-rut spills
    Where leaves have sunk their barges.

No freshet in a hollow brake
    Utters its shy cold fears,
Only the chiming sheep-bells make
    One Sabbath of the years.

The Shepherd's Hut

The smear of blue peat smoke
That staggered on the wind and broke,
The only sign of life,
Where was the shepherd's wife,
Who left those flapping clothes to dry,
Taking no thought for her family?
For, as they bellied out
And limbs took shape and waved about,
I thought, She little knows
    That ghosts are trying on her children's clothes.

At Amberley Wild Brooks

Watching the horses stand
And bend their long heads Roman-nosed
With thick cheek veins exposed,
So close to where the brook's bank shelves
They almost meet themselves
In the smooth water sliding by,
I think it strange creatures so great
Can be shut in by wooden gate
And brook no deeper than my hand,
And not like Pegasus shoot wings and fly.

By a British Barrow in War-time

Let me lie down beside you, prince,
And share – no, do not wince –
Your grave for a short hour at noon
Shaped, with molehills for stars, like the full moon.

Man in this moon of turf and chalk,
If you can hear me talk
And understand a Saxon stranger,
Listen! to-day our country is in danger.

Does that not stir you, man of bones?
Your country it was once,
Yours when you strode across these downs
Where walls still wave about your hill-top towns.

Or is the news stale in your world
where hosts are hourly hurled?
Perhaps you learnt from one of these
Who by his death gained a victorious peace.

You do not hear, man in this moon;
The skylarks might as soon

Hear me as you who are not there;
I waste breath that were precious now in prayer.

Hymn

Lord, by whose breath all souls and seeds are living
    With life that is and life that is to be,
First-fruits of earth we offer with thanksgiving
    For fields in flood with summer's golden sea.

Lord of the earth, accept these gifts in token
    Thou in thy works are to be all-adored,
From whom the light as daily bread is broken,
    Sunset and dawn as wine and milk are poured.

Poor is our praise, but these shall be our psalter;
    Lo, like thyself they rose up from the dead;
Lord, give them back when at thy holy altar
    We feed on thee, who are the living bread.

Gerard Young
(1912–1972)

Although not a poet, Gerard Young's evocation of ancient Downland is highly poetic. He reminds us of the pagan past, when St Wilfrid landed at Apuldram, surrounded by the impenetrable Andredswald, to convert to Christianity tribal cannibals.

The Mysterious Weald

This is rather a mysterious time of the year in this part of the country. If I were to take you one evening up one of those muddy broken tracks that lead to the top of the Downs and we went plunging on through the tangled bracken and slippery grass, we would eventually find ourselves on a frosty ridge overlooking a twilit world that sprawls eight hundred feet below; a dark country between the North and South Downs that with the coming of Christmas draws down over itself the murky cloak of Legend. This is the Sussex Weald, an ancient country of secret places, hidden villages, river sources, silent pools, dim glades and forgotten roads, all of them localities where in these darkening days Legend rears itself, taking advantage of the shadows of a winter's dusk.

I could point out to you the black horizon of the Forest Range within whose damp and twisted depths a monster dwells, some mighty worm that men in other days swore rose before them hideous in the evening mists. Somewhere in those woods is a straight avenue called Mike Mills' Race and here one night Mike, a smuggler mad with terror, ran a race against the Devil and the stake in the contest was his own poor Soul. All the legends are like that, full-blooded affairs laid in thoroughly haunted situations. This is the countryside where the Devil leaves his footprints in the downland turf, spits on the blackberries on October 10th and is called 'He' out of inverted respect by those who do not wish to have truck with him. Particularly round this area of Sussex are the hauntings at their height. Though eastwards at Brede they had a child-eating ogre and a nine-foot ghost of a drummer on the ramparts of Hurstmonceaux, here to the westward we prefer the macabre. We have our Kingley Vale, just over there in the Downs behind Chichester, a valley in which lie dead Danish kings, a place which at dusk on days like these is transformed into a 'sinister and fantastic forest, a home for witchcraft and unquiet spirits'. On the other side of the hills at Midhurst, Cowdray Castle is thoroughly under the monks' curse, and along the coast on stormy nights you can hear the ghastly tolling of the stolen bells of Bosham ringing out beneath the sea. The Golden Calf is buried under the Trundle mound at Goodwood and guarded by the Devil. If a branch falls in the Birdless Grove at Chichester someone dies, and four miles away from here, nearer Littlehampton, there is a pool of unknown depth called the Knucker's Hole. Something malevolent lives in the still water.

The Prayer of St Richard of Chichester

Thanks be to Thee, my Lord Jesus Christ,
For all the benefits which Thou has given me,
For all the pains and insults which Thou has borne for me.
O most merciful Redeemer, Friend, and Brother,
May I know Thee more clearly,
Love Thee more dearly,
And follow Thee more nearly.

The Furrowed Earth of England

One afternoon, just at the beginning of an autumn when the days were still and the chimney smoke rose straight and blue against the dark background of the woods, I took a small boy on a tour of inspection of some Sussex farmland.

We crossed a field, went down a dip and paused at a stile. On the other side of the stile wheat had been growing, but now the harvest was over and the stubble had been partially ploughed. The boy was interested in the long, straight furrows. He had spent most of his short life abroad and the sight of so much plough-turned earth was new to him. He looked at the long ridges, at the half-circle of furrows at the end of the field where the ploughman had turned round to go back again and then he said to me: 'Why do they do this? Is it to make it look like England?'

I never forgot that earnest question. It was so simple, yet he had struck at the very heart of Britain. In his European picture-books, in foreign newspapers, he had seen photos of the English countryside, of the horse-teams ploughing the slopes, and in a pigeon hole of his young mind this furrowed earth was the symbol of England. I believe I told him he was right.

from First Vision of Light

Swift I ran,
For they beckon'd to me
Remote by the Sea,
Saying: Each grain of Sand,
Every Stone on the Land,
Each rock & each hill,
Each fountain & rill,
Each herb & each tree,
Mountain, hill, earth & sea,
Cloud, Meteor & Star,
Are Men Seen Afar.

William Blake
Felpham
Sussex
September 1800

'Sussex is certainly a happy place and Felpham in particular is the sweetest spot on earth.'